2002
SALT LAKE CITY

MEMORABLE PHOTOGRAPHS AND STORIES FROM THE GAMES OF 2002

BY THE DESERET NEWS STAFF • PHOTOGRAPHS EDITED BY TOM SMART
TEXT EDITED BY LEE BENSON AND RAY GRASS
BOOK DESIGN BY CORY MAYLETT

Deseret News

JEFFREY D. ALLRED

Printed by Fenske Media Corporation
Rapid City, South Dakota

Library of Congress Control Number: 2002141122 • ISBN 0-913062-23-5 • ISBN 0-913062-24-3

Cover photo by Tom Smart

SCOTT G. WINTERTON

TABLE OF Contents
2002 • SALT LAKE CITY

4: INTRODUCTION

6: TORCH RELAY

10: OPENING CEREMONY

20: ALPINE SKIING

30: FREESTYLE SKIING

36: CROSS COUNTRY & BIATHLON

46: NORDIC JUMPING & COMBINED

54: FIGURE SKATING

62: ICE HOCKEY

72: SNOWBOARDING

80: SPEEDSKATING

90: SLIDING SPORTS

100: CURLING

104: OLYMPIC SCENES

116: CLOSING CEREMONY

124: RESULTS

LAURA SEITZ

2002 GAMES
Introduction
STORIES & PHOTOGRAPHS

FROM 78 COUNTRIES THEY CAME, armed with skis, skates, sleds, sticks, stones, boards and biathlon rifles. Some were from places where it's almost always winter, a few were from places where it hasn't snowed since the last Ice Age. In all there were 2,526 of them, winter Olympians by definition and qualification, chasing 234 medals in the mountains and valleys of Salt Lake. For 17 days in February they chased them; 17 days Salt Lake won't soon forget.

The numbers help define the spectacle: as many as 4 billion television viewers worldwide… 1.6 million tickets sold… 70,000 visitors to the Olympic corridor a day… 15,000-seat grandstands at the venues routinely filled to capacity… 400,000 hotdogs consumed—in just the first week… 25,000 volunteers… 15,000 security personnel… $885 a seat for a ticket to opening and closing ceremonies… $550 for a ticket to see the ladies figure skating final, with scalpers getting five times that on the street.

But the XIX Olympic Winter Games held in the biggest metropolitan area in Winter Games history were more than the best-attended, most-watched, tightest-secured and highest-priced in history. They were also filled with arguably the most variety of any Winter Games ever.

Opposite page: Snowboarder Isabelle Franc of France is all form and focus as she races to gold.

These were the Games of Croatian alpine skier Janica Kostelic, just 20, winning an unprecedented four medals, one more than even the great Killy.

These were the Games of a Harry Potter look-alike from Switzerland named Simon Ammon magically flying to two jumping gold medals, the first international triumphs of his life.

These were the Games of Norwegian biathlete Ole Einar Bjoerndalen, a golden winner in every race. Norway hasn't had to use skiing soldiers since the days of the Birkebeiner, but if the need arises, they've got Bjoerndalen.

These were the Games when Canada wiped out 50 years of Olympic frustration and won not one but two gold medals in hockey, its birthright sport.

These were the Games of a figure skating controversy involving a French judge, Russian stylists, Canadian perfectionists and American ice.

These were the Games of a Finnish dual threat named Samppa Lajunen who mined an unprecedented three golds, the maximum, in nordic combined.

These were the Games that saw a united Germany, 13 years from the fall of the wall, win a Winter Games record 35 medals—two more than the most the West and East ever managed back in the Cold War days when they each got to send a team.

These were the Games of Australia's first-ever wintertime gold medals, one by an aerialist who had the air of her life and one by a short tracker who had the luck of his life.

These were the Games of the fastest -- and highest, at 4,675 feet—speedskating track in history, and the slowest—and highest, at 5,882 feet—cross country course in history.

And much to the delight of the home town crowd, these were the Games when the United States of America, always a bridesmaid in the winter, broke out for 34 medals, 14 more than anyone's wildest projection and 21 more than anytime in history. If it wasn't the X-Gamers sweeping the men's snowboarding medals in halfpipe and adding an additional women's gold it was Chris Klug, a liver transplant survivor, medaling in snowboarding's parallel race, or Jill Bakken and Vonetta Flowers winning the first-ever women's bobsled race, or Todd Hays and his crew and Brian Shimer and his crew taking silver-bronze in men's bobsled, wiping out 46 years of American frustration, or Chris Witty, barely out of bed from a case of mono, winning speedskating gold in world record time, or Sarah Hughes winning the ladies figure skating title, giving her quite a souvenir to pack home to close out her junior year in high school, or Apolo Anton Ohno bringing the odd sport of short track into the national vocabulary.

Nowhere was the variety any more evident than a USA team that awarded medals to the first Mexican-American (speedskater Derek Parra), the first Cuban-American (speedskater Jennifer Rodriguez) and the first African-American gold medalist (bobsledder Flowers) in Winter Games history.

Not to mention the first third-generation U.S. Olympian—skeleton racer Jim Shea—who, like his grandfather in 1932, won gold.

All of this was watched live by a captive Utah audience mesmerized by a sporting spectacle of largely unexpected power and proportion.

From the lighting of the flame at opening ceremonies—by members of the 1980 U.S. gold medal hockey team—to the downtown medals ceremonies in front of 20,000 that kick-started nightly rock concerts, to the mountain fireworks display at closing ceremonies, the stage was the athlete's in the Games of Salt Lake. For 17 days they owned the place.

TOM SMART

SCOTT G. WINTERTON

Left: *After a sunrise ceremony performed under Delicate Arch by her Northern Ute grandfather, Stephanie LaRee Spann, 16, starts the Olympic flame on its journey through Utah.*

Above: *LDS Pres. Gordon B. Hinckley lifts the torch.*

Above right: *George DiCarlo, a gold medal swimmer in the L.A. Games, exits the Glenwood Springs, Colo. pool after backstroking his leg of the relay.*

Near right: *LaVell Edwards, who else?, carries the torch into LaVell Edwards Stadium.*

Far right: *Mary Geraghty, who lost her firefighter husband, Edward, in the 9-11 attack, holds the flame at Ground Zero.*

SCOTT G. WINTERTON

CHAPTER **One**

TORCH RELAY

FOR A MEMORABLE 65 DAYS, through 46 states and 13,500 miles, the Olympic flame made its way across America to Salt Lake, stopping more times than a senior citizen bus tour. Eleven thousand five hundred torchbearers carried the torch two-tenths of a mile at a time as millions stood to the side of the road, or the river, or the mountain, to watch and applaud a tradition older than any of us.

Ignited by the sun's rays in a ceremony in Olympia, Greece, on Nov. 19, 2001, the Olympic flame first made its way across Greece, birthplace of the Games, to Athens, where it was airlifted to Atlanta. There, at the site of the 1996 Centennial Olympics, Muhammad Ali, a gold medalist in Rome, passed the flame to Olympic figure skating champion Peggy Fleming and her coach, Bob Paul, and the world's most emotional relay was officially underway.

Barely three months from the terrorist tragedies of Sept. 11, the torch made healing stops in Washington, D.C., where President Bush helped pass it along, and New York City, spending Christmas there after a ferry boat filled with 14 people who had either lost loved ones or saved lives on Sept. 11 circled the torch around the Statue of Liberty.

Torchbearers ranged from the young to the old, from the famous to the not-as-famous; most were nominated for the inspiration they'd provided to others. In

STUART JOHNSON

LAURA SEITZ

TORCH RELAY

Kansas City, 12-year-old twin girls carried the torch together—the one with cerebral palsy and the sister who had nominated her because she was so brave.

Former prisoners of war carried the torch, cancer survivors carried the torch, moms and dads and people who had been married 77 years carried the torch. Sports heroes David Robinson and Lance Armstrong helped it along, as did Tom Hanks and Madeleine Albright. Teresa Earnhardt carried it in memory of her late husband Dale, Olympians Rulon Gardner and Billy Mills carried it and gold medal swimmer George DiCarlo swam with it in a pool in Colorado using a one-handed backstroke.

Day by day, mile by mile, the flame from Olympia made its way, helped along by train, plane, car, dogsled, boat, canoe, wheelchair, stagecoach, bicycle, snowmobile, ice skates and plenty of running shoes. The torch made a loop around the Indianapolis Speedway and hitched along with a cattle drive in Texas and hopped a plane in Seattle for a day-trip in Alaska. At Squaw Valley, Calif., site of the 1960 Winter Games, it went on a ski run.

It entered Utah at Delicate Arch, ushered in by a Northern Ute named Frank Arrowchis who performed a sunrise ceremony "to bless the Olympic future" and then pointed his granddaughter Stephanie LaRee Spann down the trail toward Olympic City.

More than 1,100 Utahns took the flame through 50 cities and towns. In Parowan, 93-year-old Carol Wright, a cousin to Alma Richards, Utah's first gold medalist, helped it along. In Provo, LaVell Edwards carried the flame. In Salt Lake, four-time Olympian L. Jay Sylvester trotted it down the Capitol steps. Civic leaders Spence Eccles and Jon Huntsman carried the torch and LDS President Gordon B. Hinckley passed it along. Basketball gold medalists Karl Malone, John Stockton and Natalie Williams were part of the procession, along with hundreds more, all with their own slightly more private stories and accomplishments.

By the time the flame reached downtown Salt Lake on Feb. 7 for its final rest before lighting the Olympic Stadium caldron, 50,000 people had made their way to Washington Square, there to pay homage to a flame that has flickered but always sprang back to life for the past 2,778 years. In a world of uncertainty, few icons exist with more promise and warmth. Or, as the Salt Lake Torch Relay showed, with more people willing to pass it along.

TOM SMART

TOM SMART

Left: *Silhouetted by a neon Stars & Stripes, crowds gather on the grounds of the Utah State Capitol to greet the Olympic flame.*

Above: *With her husband, Salt Lake Organizing Committee President Mitt Romney, looking on Ann Romney transfers the flame in Salt Lake City.*

Right: *The Olympic flame gets a Utah State Parks boat escort across the Great Salt Lake.*

Far right: *Janet Whitesell and her Alaskan Huskies carry the torch through Gallatin County, Mont.*

Below: *Marion Winn, married to Erma for 77 years, lights the caldron at the State Capitol.*

Lower right: *Flags from all nations welcome the flame.*

RAVELL CALL

MICHAEL BRANDY

TOM SMART

JOHANNA WORKMAN

9

TOM SMART

SCOTT G. WINTERTON

Opposite page: The Child of Light segment features skaters in elaborate costumes.

Above: Athletes from 78 nations flank the Utah Symphony and Mormon Tabernacle Choir.

Right: John Glenn, front right, Desmond Tutu, Cathy Freeman, Steven Spielberg, Lech Walesa, Kazuyoshi Funaki, Jean-Claude Killy and Jean-Michel Cousteau carry the Olympic flag.

TOM SMART

CHAPTER
Two
OPENING CEREMONY

'ON BEHALF of a proud, determined and grateful nation, I declare open the Games of Salt Lake City, celebrating the Olympic Winter Games."

With these words, delivered by President George W. Bush on a crisp, clear Friday February in Rice-Eccles Olympic Stadium, the 19th Olympic Winter Games officially began on Feb. 8, 2002.

Salt Lake's Games opened amid the usual pomp, ceremony and emotion that traditionally attends such an affair... and then some. With the nation and world still mindful of the September 11th terrorists attacks that threatened to derail the Games, and with Utahns especially mindful of the long decades spent in preparing for this moment, the ensuing opening ceremony was a mixture of homage to the past, a celebration of the present—and metal detectors at every entrance.

Undeterred by neither $885 ticket prices nor the metal detectors, a sellout crowd of more than 55,000 came early to clear security in plenty of time to see the arrival of the tattered but still waving American flag rescued from the World Trade Center Sept. 11 rubble. A combination of New York City firemen, policemen and U.S. Olympians carried the flag into the stadium as the Mormon Tabernacle Choir sang the national anthem.

And the crowd stayed on, thrilling to the parade of

11

nations as more than 2,500 athletes from 78 nations filed in wearing their national uniforms, including a Bermudan in shorts; mesmerized by a thrilling "Child of Light" cultural show representing the theme of the 19th Games "Light the Fire Within," in awe when the Olympic flag arrived carried by a world-community cast of Steven Spielberg, John Glenn, Desmond Tutu, Lech Walesa, Cathy Freeman, Jean-Michael Cousteau, Jean-Claude Killy and Kazuyoshi Funaki, and, last but far from least, witnessed the surprise lighting of the caldron by 18 members of the 1980 "Miracle On Ice" United States hockey team. With that, the Games were really on.

STUART JOHNSON

JEFFREY D. ALLRED

TOM SMART

Far left: As fireworks flare above the athletes, the Olympic rings light up on the stadium floor below.

Left: A train commemorating the linking of the transcontinental railroad in Utah rides into opening ceremonies, without a track in sight.

Above: An honor guard of New York City Firefighters, Policemen and U.S. Olympians carefully carry the flag rescued from Ground Zero into Olympic Stadium in preparation for the national anthem.

TOM SMART

Left: *An acrobatic ice skater leaves a trail of fireworks.*

Below: *Skaters parade flags representing cities that have hosted the 19 Olympic Winter Games.*

Bottom: *Presidents Rogge, Romney and Bush acknowledge the crowd.*

TOM SMART

TOM SMART

TOM SMART

GERRY AVANT

LAURA SEITZ

Far left: *Native Americans parade in traditional dress as they welcome the world to their home.*

Above: *President George W. Bush shares a laugh with U.S. Olympic athletes prior to officially opening the Games of Salt Lake.*

Left: *With their parents asleep, pioneer children imagine their place in a dreamland abundant with deer, bear and wild horses.*

Opposite page: *Children of Light hold their lanterns high, symbolically lighting the way for humanity to follow.*

LAURA SEITZ

LAURA SEITZ

JOHANNA WORKMAN

TOM SMART

STUART JOHNSON

LAURA SEITZ

Opposite, top left: *Sting and Yo-Yo Ma perform.*

Opposite, top center: *The Child of Light battles through a metaphorical storm representing life and all its adversities.*

Opposite, top right: *After performing the national anthem and Olympic Hymn, members of the Tabernacle Choir and Utah Symphony enjoy the best seats in the stadium.*

Bottom left: *Five ice skaters perform within the boundaries of the interlocking Olympic rings.*

Above: *In the rendezvous portion of the entertainment, pioneer settlers cut loose and celebrate.*

Right: *Organizing President Mitt Romney welcomes and salutes the world.*

Far right: *A skater, one of 25 wearing windless, dove-like kites, floats as if above the ice as a symbol of peace.*

TOM SMART

JEFFREY D. ALLRED

17

STUART JOHNSON

JEFFREY D. ALLRED

TOM SMART

TOM SMART

JOHANNA WORKMAN

Opposite page: *Mike Eruzione, captain of the 1980 United States hockey team, holds the torch high as he and his "Miracle On ice" teammates prepare to light the Olympic caldron.*

Above left: *The Journey West: performers pay homage to pioneer families who followed their dreams.*

Bottom left: *The fire within consumes the Olympic rings after the caldron has been lighted.*

Left: *With Picabo Street leading the cheers, U.S. athletes cavort during the Parade of Nations.*

Top right: *A bigger-than-life slide show lights up the stadium.*

Above: *Athletes from Germany enter the Stadium. German athletes went on to garner the highest number of total medals.*

19

JOHANNA WORKMAN

Opposite page: Going all out all the time, Bode Miller was never boring as he raced from behind to two alpine silver medals.

Right: Croatia's Janica Kostelic holds her skis aloft after winning the women's slalom, collecting her third of four alpine medals.

Below: It's all downhill gold for Austria's Fritz Strobl.

JOHANNA WORKMAN

CHAPTER
Three
ALPINE SKIING

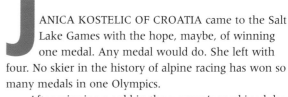

JOHANNA WORKMAN

JANICA KOSTELIC OF CROATIA came to the Salt Lake Games with the hope, maybe, of winning one medal. Any medal would do. She left with four. No skier in the history of alpine racing has won so many medals in one Olympics.

After winning a gold in the women's combined, her first event, she went on to win golds in giant slalom and slalom and a silver in super-G. She did not ski in the downhill.

Starting with a win in the combined event—a competition that combines downhill and slalom—not only gave Kostelic the victory she said she most coveted, but it seemed to provide the foundation of confidence for winning three more medals. "After I won the medal, the pressure was off. I could relax," she said in a press conference immediately after winning the combined. "If (winning more medals) happens, it's good, and if it doesn't, it's good again. I don't need another medal."

Coming into the Games, few would have given her much hope of winning. She underwent major surgery on her left knee just 10 months before the Olympics. Two months before the Olympics she was skiing and living with pain.

"She did a smart choice," said Anja Paerson of Sweden, who won a silver in the giant slalom and a bronze in the slalom. "She stopped World Cup (racing) to train a little bit and get through her injuries. I could see her today, she's a much happier skier than two months ago."

Her historic accomplishments are all the more meaningful given her skiing background. When Kostelic and her brother, Ivica, began racing, money was short. When they traveled they slept in a car and ate salami and pickle sandwiches. She said it wasn't so bad, "It was like camping," but it was hardly the usual skier's road to fame and glory.

Then, two years ago, at the age of 18, she became the second youngest skier ever to win a World Cup overall title.

Her brother, Ivica, might have added to the family's medal haul. He was heavily favored in the men's Olympic slalom, along with American Bode Miller from Franconia, N.H., but both skiers fell on their second runs.

Carole Montillet of France also took a pre-Olympic break. Two weeks before the Games she went to San Diego, trained on the beach and got her mind back on skiing. Then she came to Utah and won gold in the downhill.

There were others in these Olympics who found that success bred success. Kjetil Andre Aamodt of Norway said after winning the men's combined that "The pressure was off." He went on to win gold in the men's super-G.

Miller, America's only medal winner in the alpine events, also alluded to the fact that winning one medal made it easier to win his second. It was Miller's rodeo-style skiing that led to both his successes—silver medals in men's combined and giant slalom—as well as his crash in the slalom. Skiers talked and joked about Miller's wild, off-balance style, but no one disputed the fact that when he survives he's the fastest technical skier in the world.

After living in the shadow of teammate Hermann Maier, Stephan Eberharter of Austria took center stage as Maier was injured in a motorcycle accident and could not attend the Games. A silver medalist in the giant slalom four years earlier in Nagano to Maier's gold, Eberharter took advantage of Maier's absence in Salt Lake and won GS gold. Earlier, the Austrian collected silver in the super-G and bronze in the downhill.

Lasse Kjus of Norway was another double medal winner. He won silver in the downhill and bronze in the GS. Renate Goetschl of Austria won two medals, bronze in the downhill and silver in the combined.

Along with the success stories, there were disap-

pointments, many of them coming from the U.S. Ski Team.

Daron Rahlves of Sugar Bowl, Calif., a favorite in the super-G and considered a top challenger in the downhill, had what he called "disappointing" races. In the downhill he played it "cautiously" and finished 16th. And in the super-G, where he was a strong favorite, he made mistakes midway down the course and finished 8th.

Caroline Lalive of Truckee, Calif., considered another possible medal winner, fell three times in three races, the third time after only 13 seconds on the course.

Picabo Street of Park City announced she was retiring after a disappointing 16th in the downhill. The silver medalist in downhill in Lillehammer and gold medalist in super-G in Nagano battled back from injury to compete on home snow, but faded at the end of her run.

The alpine events in Salt Lake's Olympics showcased the veterans of the sport—Kjus, Aamodt, Eberharter and Sonja Nef (bronze medalist in the GS)—as well as the rising new stars—Kostelic, Paerson and Miller—all of whom figure to be back in four more years.

JOHANNA WORKMAN

JOHANNA WORKMAN

JOHANNA WORKMAN

RAVELL CALL

SALT LAKE 2002

RAVELL CALL

Opposite page: *Stephan Eberharter of Austria falls flat on the snow as he realizes he's won gold in the men's GS.*

Far left: *Jean-Pierre Vidal of France rejoices after winning the men's slalom.*

Left: *Austrian coach Robert Trenkwalder is overcome with emotion after Austria wins gold and bronze in men's downhill.*

Top: *U.S. team member Kristina Koznick races past a gate in the women's GS.*

Above center: *Flags wave at Snowbasin.*

23

JOHANNA WORKMAN

SCOTT G. WINTERTON

Left: With the rocky peaks of Snowbasin as a backdrop, Janica Kostelic goes low to get super-G gold.

Above: Jonna Mendes of the U.S. blows kisses to crowd after women's super-G.

JOHANNA WORKMAN

Above: Men's combined medalists Bode Miller, left, Kjetil Andre Aamodt and Benjamin Raich hold their victory flowers high.

Right: In her last race, Picabo Street negotiates Snowbasin's Wildflower downhill course.

Far right: Street embraces U.S. teammate Jonna Mendes as Picabo concludes her storied career.

TOM SMART

JEFFREY D. ALLRED

25

TOM SMART

TOM SMART

TOM SMART

JOHANNA WORKMAN

JOHANNA WORKMAN

Far left: *U.S. downhill hopeful Daron Rahlves loses balance on the Flintlock Jump.*

Center top: *At the bottom of Snowbasin's slalom course, skiers are greeted by an amphitheater of spectators.*

Center: *Kjetil Andre Aamodt looks to the scoreboard to verify his win in men's combined.*

Center bottom: *Stephan Eberharter of Austria carves a tight turn en route to men's GS gold.*

Above: *Double-gold medalist Kjetil Andre Aamodt celebrates.*

Opposite: *Janica Kostelic flashes a golden smile after winning her third gold medal of the Games, this one in women's GS.*

CHUCK WING

Below: *Croatian Janica Kostelic wins the women's downhill.*

Bottom: *Austria's Benjamin Raich rejoices with a bronze finish in men's combined.*

Right: *Truls Ove Karlsen of Norway is dejected after falling in men's combined.*

Far right: *Fritz Strobl of Austria carries away the spoils after winning in men's downhill.*

JOHANNA WORKMAN

JOHANNA WORKMAN

JOHANNA WORKMAN

RAVELL CALL

TOM SMART

JOHANNA WORKMAN

Above: *With eyes closed and fist in the air, America's Bode Miller realizes he's won a silver medal in the men's GS at Park City.*

Above right: *Gold medalist Kjetil Andre Aamodt of Norway goes airborne on the downhill portion of the men's combined.*

Right: *Czech Lucie Hrstkova at high velocity races down the Women's Olympic Super-G at Snowbasin.*

JOHANNA WORKMAN

29

LAURA SEITZ

FREESTYLE SKIING

JASON OLSON

CHAPTER
Four
FREESTYLE SKIING

IN A MATTER OF A FEW SECONDS, Alisa Camplin forgot about the leech-filled pond in Australia and the pain of injuries, and focused on the piece of gold hanging around her neck.

No one was more surprised to see it there than the 27-year-old Camplin. Up to this moment she had won nothing of world significance in her lifetime.

But her backward takeoff, followed by two flips with three twists, was perfectly executed, right down to the landing. Quietly she whispered "please, please, please" as she watched the scoreboard. Then came the tears and uncontrollable excitement. She had won.

The 5-foot-2 blonde from Australia had bettered an international field of aerial giants to win the Olympic gold.

The trip to Salt Lake in itself was a Cinderella story. At 19, and a non-skier, she watched on TV as aerialists twisted and turned in the air. As a former gymnast, she was captivated. She found her way to the Australian Olympic Winter Sports Institute, where the staff took her in and taught her the tricks before they taught her to ski.

Her training site was a green-colored pond near town where fish were planted to try and control the leeches. Then there were the injuries, which included a broken collarbone, broken hand, separated shoulder, torn Achilles tendon and nine concussions. Doctors recommended she quit.

Instead, she persevered and her reward was the first gold medal ever won in the Winter Olympics by an

LAURA SEITZ

LAURA SEITZ

Top: Competitors called Deer Valley's aerial jump among the finest ever built.

Above: *After a crash landing, Canada's Steve Omischl collapses in the landing area.*

Right: *Crowd favorite Jonny "Dinner Roll" Moseley.*

Opposite: *Park City's own Joe Pack gets a silver medal hug from his brother, Tim.*

Australian woman.

In men's aerials, Ales Valenta of the Czech Republic knew one thing before going into his final jump. His choice of jumps was, to put it mildly, a gamble. In all his airtime, he had only landed his signature jump—a double full-double full-full—twice.

The three-time Olympian made it three when he hit five twists and three somersaults perfectly.

The jump landed him in first place with but one skier yet to jump, the formidable Eric Bergoust of Missoula, Mont., defending gold medalist and leader after the first round of jumps.

Bergoust fell back on landing his second jump, however. "I put too much energy into my takeoff," the normally clutch performer said. He dropped from 1st to 12th.

It was Joe Pack who came through for his hometown of Park City. He connected with the crowd and his jumps to earn silver.

On the mogul hill, it was defending gold medalist Jonny Moseley of Tiburon, Calif., who stole the hearts from the crowd but not votes from the judges. The skier who introduced the world to the "heli-mute grab" four years ago in Nagano and won the gold pulled out a new jump called the "dinner roll" for the Salt Lake Games. Although Moseley executed the trick expertly, judges considered it only the fourth best performance of the day.

It was Janne Lahtela of Finland who put down the fastest run and the best scores for his two jumps to take the gold. Lahtela was a silver medalist behind Moseley in 1998. Silver medalist was Travis Mayer of Steamboat Springs, Colo., a rookie on the World Cup circuit who finished only four-tenths of a point behind Lahtela.

In women's moguls, Kari Traa of Norway came in as the odds-on favorite and she left that way as well. She breezed through qualifying and then scored high marks in the air and ski time through the bumps to beat out Shannon Bahrke of Reno, Nev.

Tae Satoya of Japan, the gold medalist in 1998, finished with the bronze.

Both the aerials and moguls, contested at Deer Valley Resort, proved crowd favorites. And with three medals for the U.S. Ski and Snowboard Team, among the most successful.

LAURA SEITZ

JOHANNA WORKMAN

LAURA SEITZ

FREESTYLE SKIING

LAURA SEITZ

LAURA SEITZ

Opposite top: *U.S. mogul skier Evan Dybvig screams in pain after falling in qualification round.*

Opposite left: *Czech Ales Valenta flips for gold.*

Opposite right: *Alisa Camplin of Australia can't believe she's just jumped into first place.*

Above: *Travis Mayer of the United States exults over his silver medal finish in men's moguls.*

Center: *Men's aerialist champ Ales Valenta applauds the crowd for applauding him.*

Top right: *Rough landing costs defending Olympic aerial champ Eric Berguost another gold medal.*

Bottom right: *Women's mogul silver medalist Shannon Bahrke of the U.S. lets out a cheer.*

RAVELL CALL

LAURA SEITZ

33

FREESTYLE SKIING

LAURA SEITZ

RAVELL CALL

Top: *Canadian aerial medalists Veronica Brenner (5) and Deidra Dionne (3) flank Australian gold medalist Alisa Camplin.*

Above: *U.S.A. moguls fans at Deer Valley let their colors show.*

Right: *Jonny Moseley's executes his "Dinner roll."*

Far right: *Shannon Bahrke wins silver for the U.S. in women's moguls.*

RAVELL CALL

LAURA SEITZ

RAVELL CALL

Above: *Wearing his lucky 13 bib, "Jumpin'" Joe Pack lets loose after jumping to his aerials silver medal.*

Right: *Aussie Alisa Camplin turned it around to win her country's first women's Olympic Winter Games gold medal.*

LAURA SEITZ

35

TOM SMART

TOM SMART

TOM SMART

Left: *Mikhail Ivanov of Russia stops for a shower during the men's 50K classic race. Ivanov won gold.*

Top: *King Ole: Norway's Ole Einar Bjoerndalen waves to the crowd after winning biathlon gold.*

Above: *Norwegian fans had plenty to cheer about at the biathlon venue, where Bjoerndalen kept them happy by winning four gold medals.*

CROSS COUNTRY & BIATHLON

TOM SMART

CHAPTER
Five
CROSS COUNTRY & BIATHLON

TOM SMART

AT THE oxygen-thin altitude of 5,882 feet—more than a mile above sea level and the highest in Olympic Winter Games history—there was some speculation there might be a new world order at the Soldier Hollow cross country venue. Maybe even the Americans would crash the party.

But there wasn't a new world order. All the usual suspects came to the forefront, with athletes from the traditional cross country strongholds of Norway and Russia dominating, followed by the always-there Italians.

Unfortunately, something else didn't change either. The cloud of performance-enhancing drug use that has plagued the sport continued to hang low as three medal-winning skiers were expelled from the

Left: *As her teammates hug, Switzerland's Natascia Cortesi Leonardi celebrates a bronze finish in the women's relay by somersaulting across the snow.*

Above: *Spectator Patricia Kimball has 5-ring focus.*

37

Games after testing positive for darbepoetin, a drug that promotes the production of oxygen-carrying red blood cells.

The Olympic expulsions came on the heels of a doping scandal at the 2001 World Nordic Championships in Lahti, Finland, where six members of the Finnish team tested positive and were suspended. That effectively ended the Finn's Olympic hopes—no Finnish racers placed on the Salt Lake podium—but it didn't deter Russian women Larissa Lazutina and Olga Danilova and Spain's Johann Muehlegg from following in the cheater's tracks.

Lazutina, Danilova and the German-born Muehlegg, who switched his allegiance to Spain in 1999 after a dispute with the German cross country team, tested positive for darbepoetin in tests conducted the last two days of the Games. The results came in time to strip Muehlegg of gold in the men's 50K and Lazutina of gold in the women's 30K but too late to prevent Muehlegg from going home with golds captured earlier in the 30K and 10K pursuit, Lazutina with silvers in pursuit and the 15K and Danilova with gold in pursuit and silver in the 10K.

JASON OLSON

Despite going through doping control after winning these earlier medals, the three skiers somehow escaped detection. Since Olympic rules do not allow for retroactive suspensions, Muehlegg, Lazutina and Danilova each left with two medals hanging from their necks—a sixth of all the cross country medals awarded at Soldier Hollow.

The downer cast by the closing drug busts was in sharp contrast to the nearly perfect cross country weather and spirited racing during much of the fortnight. Unlike cross country courses in Scandinavia and Europe that are typically thickly forested, Soldier Hollow's wide open spaces afforded exceptional spectating to the largest crowds ever to witness the sport in North America.

Canada's Beckie Scott took advantage of the home snow with a bronze finish in pursuit, the first cross country medal won by a North American woman. No U.S. athletes found the podium, however, and there were no top 10 individual finishes, although the U.S.

JASON OLSON

TOM SMART

TOM SMART

Top left: Marit Bjoergen, left, of Norway and Katrin Smigun of Estonia ski past the Stars & Stripes in the women's 30K.

Far left bottom: Italy's Marianna Longa, left, congratulates her medal-winning countrywomen, Gabriella Paruzzi and Stefania Belmondo, for winning gold-silver in the women's 30K cross country race.

Left: The afternoon sun casts deep shadows on the groomed track as the women begin the 15K at Soldier Hollow.

Above: After edging Italy's Cristian Zorzi at the finish of the men's 4X10K cross country relay, Norway's Thomas Alsgaard celebrates.

Right: Nice place for a nap: Little Zatha Loewen sleeps on her father's shoulders as Eric Loewen watches cross country racing at Soldier Hollow.

TOM SMART

men's team's fifth place finish in the relay was an all-time high.

BIATHLON

Stealing the show, and that's putting it mildly, was Norway's Ole Einar Bjoerndalen, who swept the table with four golds in as many events. Only two other winter athletes have won as many golds in one Games -- Russian speedskater Lydia Skovlikova with four in 1964 and American speedskater Eric Heiden with five in 1980.

Bjoerndalen warmed up by competing in the men's cross country 30K race, finishing sixth. Then he moved on to his specialty—skiing with a rifle on his back—and got serious. He started with a win in the 20K, then a win two days later in the 10K sprint, then a win three days after that in the 12.5K pursuit and after a four-day rest—and with King Harald of Norway looking on from the stands—a final win with his Norwegian teammates in the men's relay.

German women biathletes won three of four gold medals, including the relay, while Norway's Liv Grete Poiree won two silver medals, matching the total won by France's Raphael Poiree, who captured a silver and a bronze. The husband-and-wife team became the first spouses to medal while competing for different countries. The most thrilling race of the week came in the men's relay when Norway's Thomas Alsgaard crossed the finish line 0.3 seconds, or about a ski tip, ahead of Italy's Cristian Zorzi. It was a replay of Alsgaard's photo finish win over Italy's Silvio Fauner in the relay four years before in Nagano and a reverse of the Italian's last-second relay win over the Norwegians in Lillehammer in 1994.

Most heartwarming was Estonia's breakthrough three medals, two by Andrus Veerpalu. They were the former Soviet republic's first medals.

The biggest surprise was a complete shutout for the Swedish team, including zero medals for World Cup world champion Per Elofsson, who, like much of the rest of the Swedes, was fighting sickness.

TOM SMART

Above: *Wendy Wagner of the United States steps out smartly during the women's 5K pursuit cross country race at Soldier Hollow.*

Right: *Johann Muehlegg waves Spain's flag after finishing first in the men's 10K pursuit race.*

Middle right: *As the men's biathlon relay begins, athletes line up to shoot at the first station.*

Opposite: *With the Olympic rings spurring them on, the field launches into action at the start of the men's 4X10K cross country relay race.*

TOM SMART

TOM SMART

TOM SMART

41

Above: *Wendy Wagner of the United States flies downhill during the women's 10K classical race.*

Top left: *Germany's Andrea Henkel sights in on the gold medal she would win in the women's biathlon 15K race.*

Left: *Masaaki Kosu of Japan collapses at the end of the men's 15K classical competition at Soldier Hollow.*

STUART JOHNSON

TOM SMART

Top: *Skiing on home snow, Nina Kemppel of the United States glides her way in the women's 10K classical race.*

Above: *Russia's Olga Pyleva, winner of the gold medal in women's 10K pursuit biathlon, lets out a cheer.*

Right: *Italy's Cristian Zorzi kneels in mock "I'm Not Worthy" fashion before gold medalist Tor Arne Hetland of Norway.*

TOM SMART

43

TOM SMART

44

TOM SMART

TOM SMART

STUART JOHNSON

Opposite page: Women biathletes set out as the 4X7.5K relay begins.

Top far left: America's Carl Swenson exults as he crosses the finish line, giving the U.S. fifth place in the men's cross country relay, its highest ever.

Top middle: Stefania Belmondo of Italy throws the crowd a kiss after the women's 30K. Belmondo won a silver medal, the 9th of her career.

Left: Gold medalist Andrus Veerplau of Estonia holds his flowers high.

Bottom left: Norway's Bente Skari keeps an eye on the track as she takes a drink in the 30K

Below: Germany's Claudia Kuenzel, Manuela Henkel, Evi Sachenbacher and Viola Bauer teamed for relay gold.

TOM SMART

TOM SMART

45

JEFFREY D. ALLRED

TOM SMART

TOM SMART

Opposite: Daito Takahashi of Japan soars over Utah Olympic Park in K120 nordic combined jumping.

Top: Utah's K90 and K120 hills are all lit up and ready to go.

Above: An exhausted Todd Lodwick hits the snow at the end of the nordic combined relay.

Right: Samppa Lajunen carries the Finnish flag after winning nordic combined individual gold.

STUART JOHNSON

CHAPTER **Six**
NORDIC JUMPING & COMBINED

FOR A PRIME Olympic example of peaking at just the right time, look no farther than Switzerland's Simon Ammann—and in this case, "peaking" can be taken literal. Ammann is a nordic jumper.

The 20-year-old Harry Potter look-alike came off the injured list—he'd suffered a concussion and multiple cuts and bruises in a crash six weeks before the Olympics—to dominate the jumping competition at Utah Olympic Park.

With no international credentials to portend what was to come, Ammann had the longest, highest and most stylish jumps in both the individual K90 and K120 competition as well as the team K120 competition. Only a lack of depth in the Swiss team, which finished 7th, kept him from three medals.

Ammann did all this in the shadow of two giants of the sport who came to Salt Lake at the top of their games. Poland's Adam Malysz was the defending world champion and co-favorite on both the normal and big hills alongside Germany's Sven Hannawald, fresh from a sweep of the revered Four-Hill competition. Malysz and Hannawald put plenty of pressure on the Swiss jumper, whose 133 meter jump on the K120 jump ranks as UOP's longest, but he did not crack. Hannawald and Malysz finished silver-bronze in the K90 and Malysz won silver in the K120 while Hannawald, jumping last, went for broke with the second-longest jump of the day but crashed on his landing, losing enough style points to finish fourth.

All week during the jumping competition, crowds of 20,000-plus made the mile trek to the Olympic Park hill as nordic-style jumping became a fan favorite despite the fact North American jumpers had little presence (America's best individual effort: Airborne Alan Alborn of Anchorage in 21st place). A huge crowd at the team event was rewarded with the closest competition in Olympic history. Germany defeated Finland by a tenth of a point, 974.1 to 974, as Germany's anchor jumper, Martin Schmitt, came through with jumps of 131.5 meters—the day's longest—and 123.5 meters.

NORDIC COMBINED

Finland's Samppa Lajunen did Simon Ammann

plus one in the nordic combined by winning gold in every category—individual, sprint and team.

Lajunen, 22, competed as an 18-year-old in Nagano and won silver medals in the individual and team competitions, so his emergence as king of the combined—the event that couples nordic jumping and nordic skiing—was not unexpected, particularly when reigning World Cup champion and double Nagano gold medalist Bjarte Engen Vik of Norway retired at the end of the 2001 season. The only question was how Lajunen would handle Olympic pressure and he answered that in the affirmative three times.

Spurred by the prospect of Americans possibly getting a first-ever medal in nordic combined, large crowds attended both the jumping competitions at Olympic Park and the cross country racing at Soldier Hollow.

America's best did better than ever before but at that didn't quite make the podium.

Todd Lodwick, the leading American and a frequent World Cup victor, came closest with three top 10 finishes—a pair of seventh-place efforts in the individual events and a fourth place team finish with an All-Colorado lineup that included Billy Demong, Matt Dayton and Johnny Spillane. The Colorado Americans were in third place after the first day jumping competition, behind Finland and Japan, and with a home snow advantage at the rarified air of Soldier Hollow were poised for a medal. But Germany and Austria leapfrogged them on the cross country track to finish silver-bronze behind Finland. The U.S. skied past Japan but it was only good enough for one spot away from the podium.

TOM SMART

JEFFREY D. ALLRED

Left: *Triple gold medalist Samppa Lajunen of Finland shows his form in the cross country portion of individual nordic combined.*

Above: *Swiss teammates Sylvain Freiholz, left, and Andreas Kuettel hoist a jubilant gold medalist Simon Ammann.*

JEFFREY D. ALLRED

RAVELL CALL

JEFFREY D. ALLRED

Top: *Onward and outward: Simon Ammann of Switzerland soars to gold in K120 individual jumping.*

Above: *Martin Schmitt celebrates with Team Germany after title.*

Far right: *It's all downhill for Norway's Tommy Ingebrigtsen.*

Right: *Bill Dmong of the U.S. finishes 8th in K90 nordic combined .*

JEFFREY D. ALLRED

TOM SMART

TOM SMART

JEFFREY D. ALLRED

Far left: *Finland's Samppa Lajunen throws flowers to the spectators at Soldier Hollow after winning gold in nordic combined.*

Above: *Lajunen, and his shadow, skate as one along the groomed track at Soldier Hollow.*

Left: *Media photographers move into position to take the "best" possible photos of jumpers coming off the K120 jump at the Utah Olympic Park.*

Opposite: *U.S. nordic combined athlete Johnny Spillane is tucked and ready to launch as he shoots down the K120 in-run.*

JEFFREY D. ALLRED

TOM SMART

Far right: American Bill Demong begins his descent on the long in-run leading to liftoff from the K120 nordic combined jump.

Above: Todd Lodwick leads a group of cross country skiers

Right: Germany's Sven Hannawald shows his disappointment after the top-ranked jumper fell on his second jump in the K120 competition.

Opposite: Japan's Gen Tomii is caught in the shadows of the Utah Olympic Park during his takeoff from the K90 jump in the nordic combined competition.

JASON OLSON

JEFFREY D. ALLRED

JEFFREY D. ALLRED

JASON OLSON

FIGURE SKATING

SCOTT G. WINTERTON

Left: Russia's Anton Sikharulidze and Elena Berezhnaya, right, and Canada's Jamie Sale and Dave Pelletier celebrate, for a second time, the presentation of gold medals in pairs skating.

Above: Gold medalists Sale and Pelletier were crowd favorites during exhibition performance.

Above right: Sarah Hughes, right, and her coach, Robin Wagner, show their excitement as scores are posted for ladies free skating program.

Below right: Sale and Pelletier react to their lower than expected scores.

JOHANNA WORKMAN

JOHANNA WORKMAN

CHAPTER
Seven
FIGURE SKATING

IT DIDN'T SEEM POSSIBLE that anything could overcome the current of controversy swirling around the Salt Lake Ice Center after the 2002 Olympic figure skating competition opened with a pairs event that featured the expulsion of a judge for misconduct and, in an attempt to straighten out the mess, an unprecedented awarding of double gold medals.

But then, just when it was sorely needed, redemption came from an unexpected place. When 16-year-old Sarah Hughes, a high school junior, took the ice in the ladies free skate she was in 4th place, a longshot to medal. Four minutes later, after the kind of performance that makes dreams come true, she'd given the figure skating Games something to remember other than arguing.

The near flawless performance by Hughes, a teenager without an agent, brought the regal sport back to its basics: go out, skate unencumbered and enjoy the results. The look on Hughes' face when she realized she had leapfrogged all the way to gold was the look of unadulterated—and unscripted—joy.

Exactly what figure skating needed.

To say things had started badly with the pairs is to say the French Revolution had a few shaky moments. One minute it appeared Jamie Sale and David Pelletier of Canada had clinched gold with a performance so mis-

55

JOHANNA WORKMAN

SCOTT G. WINTERTON

Left: *Tatina Navka and Roman Kostomarov of Russia capture the crowd with this segment of their performance during the ice dance competition.*

Above: *France's Marina Anissina and Gwendal Peizerat show some of their style and grace during gold-medal performance in first compulsory of their ice dance program.*

Right: *Sarah Hughes shows off her gold medal after receiving a congratulatory kiss from her dad, John, after her surprising victory in the ladies free skate program in the 2002 Games.*

CHUCK WING

Far left: *Michelle Kwan of the U.S. wipes away a tear after receiving her bronze medal in the ladies free skate.*

Left: *Kwan was much happier after hitting her jumps during earlier competition in the ladies short program at the Salt Lake Ice Center.*

Below: *Sarah Hughes receives a kiss and a gold medal from former IOC President Juan Antonio Samaranch while Kwan looks on and applauds.*

CHUCK WING

CHUCK WING

STUART JOHNSON

STUART JOHNSON

RAVELL CALL

JOHANNA WORKMAN

Far left: *Even though they didn't medal, U.S. skaters Kyoko Ina and John Zimmerman were happy with their scores in the pairs free program.*

Left: *Alexei Yagudin of Russia celebrates after completion of his gold medal performance in the men's free skate.*

Above: *John and Amy Hughes show their approval of the performance of their daughter, Sarah, in the ladies free skate.*

61

STUART JOHNSON

MICHAEL BRANDY

CHAPTER

Eight

ICE HOCKEY

Opposite: *The Russian hockey team is framed by the Olympic rings during the bronze-medal ceremonies that followed the win over Belarus.*

Above: *Kosta Krijcev holds a Macedonia and a U.S. flag in his lap as he watches a fan display a Russian flag prior to the start of the U.S./Russian semifinal hockey game.*

Right: *The Canadian women share hugs and a few tears after they beat the U.S. women in a gold-medal game played at the E Center.*

LAURA SEITZ

WHILE SPORTS HISTORIANS still debate whether the first game was played in Kingston Harbour, Ontario, in 1855 or in Windsor, Nova Scotia, in the early 1800s, there is no question ice hockey truly is Canada's game.

Which is why fans north of the border were more than a little troubled the last 50 years trying to figure out why gold had eluded them in the Olympics ever since the 1952 Winter Games in Oslo. Until that point, Canada had dominated the international hockey scene like a schoolyard bully, winning five times in the first six Games.

As 2002 approached, and with the Olympics just over the border in Utah, Canada looked to regain its title as Lord of Olympic Hockey by beefing up its national program. Former NHL legend Wayne Gretzky was named Executive Director of Team Canada and a myriad of NHL all stars the likes of Eric Lindros, Theo Fleury, Mario Lemieux, Joe Sakic, et al signed on.

After a fourth place finish in Nagano, behind the Czechs, Russians and Finns, there was no mistaking Canada was throwing everything but the Stanley Cup into the Salt Lake Games.

And while it first appeared the Canadians might have wound themselves a bit too tight—as evidenced by an opening loss to Sweden—by the end of

63

the tournament they were rolling along as if they'd invented the game, eh?

Using Gretzky's new philosophy of skill and speed rather than determination and defense, Team Canada just kept getting better as the Olympics wore on. Even the early round-robin loss to Sweden, which put Canada in line for a semifinal date in the medal round against those same Swedes, turned out to be good fortune after Belarus shocked Sweden 4–3 to open the medal round.

That enabled the Canadians, after an opening medal round win over Finland, to stay away from a loaded opposite bracket that included the Czechs, who were eliminated by Russia, and Russia, which was then eliminated in the semifinals by the United States in the first match between those two countries on American soil since the famous (or infamous if you happen to be Russian) 1980 "Miracle On Ice."

The U.S.-Russia semi had a gold-medal feel to it, with scalpers outside the E Center in West Valley City asking as much as $750 for tickets with face value a third of that.

The rematch turned out to be everything fans had

RAVELL CALL

CHUCK WING

hoped for. The U.S. jumped out to an early 3–0 lead but the Russians did not go quietly, scoring two quick goals early in the third period. Then U.S. goalie Mike Richter, under heavy attack, stingily guarded the net until the final buzzer, giving the Americans the 3–2 win.

Meanwhile, in the "other" semi the Canadians were beating a Belarus team finally out of magic by a 7–2 knockout. Thus was a dream North American gold medal match set, with the United States facing Canada for Olympic gold.

Despite home ice advantage for the U.S., Team Canada rose to the occasion more than the hosts. When Sakic scored the go-ahead goal to give Canada a 3–2 advantage just before the end of the second period, the dye was cast. Two more goals in the third clinched the 5–2 victory for the Canadians and with it the gold medal and all its attendant world neighborhood bragging rights.

Sporting his shiny new gold medal around his neck, Canadian goalie Martin Brodeur spoke for an entire country when he proudly exclaimed, "We are still a hockey power."

"A big monkey is lifted off Canada's back," agreed U.S. forward Jeremy Roenick. "This is what they have waited for, for a long time. I'm happy for them."

On the women's side of Olympic hockey, the year of Canada continued as the Canadian women upset the heavily favored Americans for the gold medal.

The U.S. team looked better than solid coming into the tournament. The women had won gold four years earlier in Nagano (over Canada), had dominated international play with 35 straight wins heading into the gold medal match, and had beaten the Canadian national women's team eight straight times.

But the Canadian women, like the men, came to Salt Lake intent on returning luster to a country where women had played hockey routinely since the late 1800s.

Determination paid off in Canada's 3–2 victory for the gold as Jayna Hefford put an exclamation point on a game the Canadians dominated from start to finish by slapping a back-breaking goal with one second remaining in the second period. Canada's Kim St. Pierre was stellar defending the goal with 25 saves on the day.

The Swedish women took the bronze medal in a victory over heavily favored Finland in Provo.

JEFFREY D. ALLRED

MICHAEL BRANDY

Opposite, top: *Members of the Canadian men's hockey team gather around the net after their win.*

Opposite, bottom: *Members of the U.S. women's hockey team wave to fans after accepting their silver medals.*

Left: *Canada's Cheryl Pounder enjoys center ice after the gold-medal match with the United States.*

Above: *Danielle Goyette holds up the Canadian flag after her team skated to a gold in the finals of women's hockey.*

65

TOM SMART

MICHAEL BRANDY

MICHAEL BRANDY

MICHAEL BRANDY

Top left: *U.S. players pour onto the ice after scoring a goal against the Russians in semifinal action at the E Center.*

Above: *Carolyn Marin, 15, shows her support for the U.S. men's hockey team.*

Far left: *Adam Deadmarsh of the U.S. team tries to get the puck past Nikolai Khabibulin of Russia.*

Left: *U.S. goalie Mike Richter makes a save against Alexei Yashin of Russia.*

Opposite: *Canadian Geraldine Heaney touches gloves with teammates after winning gold.*

MICHAEL BRANDY

67

MICHAEL BRANDY

STUART JOHNSON

STUART JOHNSON

Opposite: U.S. goalie Sara Decosta reaches out to stop a shot by Danielle Goyette of Canada in gold medal action.

Above: Aaron Miller of the U.S. team trips over his goalie, Mike Richter, after a Canadian score.

Top right: Canada's Mario Lemieux displays the flag after the gold-medal victory.

Right: Jarome Iginla, Steve Yzerman and Joe Sakic of Canada react to scoring their fourth goal against the U.S.

Far right: Iginla and Bill Guerin of the U.S. team get tangled up while fighting for control of the puck.

RAVELL CALL

RAVELL CALL

69

TOM SMART

MICHAEL BRANDY

MICHAEL BRANDY

MICHAEL BRANDY

LAURA SEITZ

MICHAEL BRANDY

Top left: *Russia's Alexei Yashin tries to slip the puck past U.S. goalie Mike Richter in the final minutes.*

Top center: *America's Brett Hull, right, waves to fans as teammate Mike Modano watches after medal ceremonies.*

Top right: *Jilyn Beglan Libby sports flags and a cell phone.*

Far left: *U.S. hockey player Shelley Looney sheds a few tears during medal ceremonies at the E Center.*

Left: *Wayne Gretzky and his wife, Janet Jones-Gretzky, are all smiles after Canada beat the U.S. for the gold medal.*

Above: *USA's Natalie Darwitz and Krissy Wendell celebrate after scoring against Finland in an early-round match.*

Opposite: *Swedish player, Mikael Renberg, is comforted by teammate after his team was upset by Berlarus.*

MICHAEL BRANDY

LAURA SEITZ

RAVELL CALL

CHAPTER **Nine**
SNOWBOARDING

THE POWER OF YOUTH was never more obvious than the snowboarding venue, where America took advantage of its own winter sports creation by winning five medals out of the 12 awarded at Park City Mountain Resort's Eagle Race Arena.

If the exact beginnings of the snowboard is hard to determine, there is no argument that a company started by America's Jake Burton in 1977 started the sport on its worldwide roll. Appropriately enough, every Salt Lake medalist but one was born after 1977 and the lone exception, giant slalom racer Chris Klug, was born in 1972.

The halfpipe medalists, including gold medalist Kelly Clark in the women's competition and Ross Powers, Danny Kass and J.J. Thomas, who went gold-silver-bronze in the men's competition, had an average age of 20, ranging from the 18-year-old Clark to Powers, the old man of the group at 23.

It all pointed to the newness of a sport that is appealing to the youth of America in record numbers and has the very real possibility of becoming a commodity America has historically lacked at the Winter Games—a signature winter sport.

In just two Olympics now, the United States has claimed six snowboarding medals—in sharp contrast to the grand total of just 29 alpine skiing medals the U.S.

Opposite: *Philipp Schoch from Switzerland carves his way down the dual giant slalom courses to win a gold in the men's competition.*

Above: *It's a long way to the bottom for the snowboarder as he begins his run in the men's giant slalom event held at the Park City Mountain Resort.*

Right: *Ueli Kestenhoz of Switzerland kicks up a wall of snow as he boards down the giant slalom course.*

SCOTT G. WINTERTON

73

has won in all 19 Winter Games.

What's more, attendance at snowboard events is not only big but loud, as was evidenced by the youthful overflow crowds that packed the stands and the standing-room areas at Park City.

Clark, a native of Mount Snow, Vermont, who switched to snowboarding from skiing at the age of 9 and never looked back, got everything started on the second full day of Olympic competition when she won gold with a nearly flawless big-air run that placed her ahead of Doriane Vidal of France and Fabienne Reuteler of Switzerland. Clark's U.S. teammates Shannon Dunn, a bronze medalist in Nagano, and Tricia Byrnes finished just out of the medals in fifth and sixth place.

As close as the women came to a sweep, the men one-upped them two days later by actually pulling it off. The one-two-three finish by Powers, Kass and Thomas was the first U.S. sweep in a Winter Games since Hayes Jenkins, Ronald Robertson and David Jenkins monopolized the podium in the 1956 Innsbruck Games in men's figure skating, and only the second U.S. medals sweep in history.

In snowboarding's parallel giant slalom event, the results were more ecumenical, with five countries represented on the podium. Frenchwomen Isabelle Blanc and Karine Ruby went gold-silver in the women's competition, followed by Lidia Trettel of Italy, while on the men's side Switzerland's Philipp Schoch was first, followed by Richard Richardsson of Sweden and Chris Klug of Aspen, Colo.

Klug's bronze medal run included a frantic repair job on the buckle of his boot just seconds before the countdown clock expired on his final run. It was a fitting, if unwelcome, bit of adversity to overcome for the 29-year-old Klug who just 18 months earlier underwent a liver transplant operation in a Denver hospital. Suffering from the same rare liver disorder that killed football great Walter Payton, Klug lost almost 30 pounds and waited 72 days in the summer of 2000 before getting a donor liver thanks to a 13-year-old gunshot victim whose family donated his organs after his death. In accepting his bronze medal, appropriately just one day after National Organ Donor Awareness Day, Klug paid tribute to those who donate organs so others may live.

"Transplants," said Klug, "save lives, cause miracles and allow dreams to be fulfilled." And he was living proof.

LAURA SEITZ

LAURA SEITZ

JASON OLSON

RAVELL CALL

Opposite: *Chris Klug of the United States gets low to the snow on his bronze-medal run in the men's snowboard giant slalom.*

Top: *Members of the National Guard take a few pictures during a break from their security duties at the Salt Lake City Games.*

Above: *Doriane Vidal of France grabs her snowboard as she gets airborne during her routine in the women's halfpipe event*

Right: *Isabelle Blanc from France plays a little tune on her snowboard for fans after winning the women's snowboard giant slalom.*

LAURA SEITZ

RAVELL CALL

Far left: Ross Powers of the U.S. completes qualification run at Park City.

Above: France's Karine Ruby and Russia's Maria Tikhvinskaya leave start gate.

Left: Powers flies high during winning routine in the men's halfpipe event.

Opposite: America's Danny Kass finishes his silver-medal run in the halfpipe.

RAVELL CALL

LAURA SEITZ

RAVELL CALL

LAURA SEITZ

CHUCK WING

Far left: *Ross Powers of the United States celebrates after a clean run in the men's halfpipe competition.*

Above: *America's Chris Klug does a fine balancing act as he boards down course en route to a bronze in the men's parallel GS.*

Left: *Kelly Clark of the United States, winner of the gold medal in the women's halfpipe event, enjoys a photo moment with silver medalist Doriane Vidal of France, right, and Fabienne Reuteler of Switzerland.*

RAVELL CALL

LAURA SEITZ

RAVELL CALL

RAVELL CALL

Top left: *Heikki Sorsa of Finland lets everyone know he wasn't happy with his performance in the men's snowboard competition.*

Above: *Brandon Weaver of Salt Lake City celebrates after the United States made a clean sweep of the medals in the men's halfpipe.*

Far left: *USA's Danny Kass, left, Ross Powers and J.J. Thomas went 1–2–3 in medals in the men's halfpipe at Park City.*

Left: *Isabelle Blanc of France is all smiles after her win in the women's parallel giant slalom.*

79

JASON OLSON

JOHANNA WORKMAN

CHAPTER Ten
SPEEDSKATING

Opposite: *Judges watch as skaters circle the track in the men's 1,000-meter short track.*

Above: *America's gold medalist Chris Witty, center, stands with Sabine Voelker of Germany and teammate Jennifer Rodriguez.*

Right: *Derek Parra of the U.S. set a world record and wins a gold medal in the men's 1,500-meter race.*

SCOTT G. WINTERTON

I N 1994 AND 1998 it was clap skates and stream-lined body suits. In 2002 speedskaters came up with yet another innovation to find more speed: the building.

The Utah Olympic Oval, a modest-looking structure with exposed rafters, quickly became the Fastest Ice on Earth during the Games of Salt Lake. In the 10 long track events—five men's and five women's—eight world records were established, 10 Olympic records, 66 national records and 193 personal records. And that's not counting the number of times records were broken and then re-broken within a matter of minutes.

Never have so many skated so fast in such little time. Ironically, the only distance that didn't see a world record was 500 meters, the shortest race and therefore the distance that figured to benefit most from the Utah Oval's oxygen-thin altitude of 4,675 feet.

The quick ice showed no favoritism. Three countries dominated the competition equally, with the United States, the Netherlands and Germany collecting eight total medals and three golds apiece. That left six medals for the rest of the world and Canada got three of those, including a gold at 500 meters from defending women's champion Catriona LeMay Doan and a bronze at 5,000 meters from Clara Hughes, a double-bronze winning cyclist at the Atlanta Games who became the fourth person in Olympic history to medal in both the summer and winter.

Dutch skater Jochem Uytdehaage was the most decorated among the men getting three medals with wins at 5,000 and 10,000 meters and a second-place finish to America's Derek Parra at 1,500 meters. Parra got silver in the 5,000 as he and Uytdehaage took turns upstaging each other by setting a world record on top of a world record.

Germany's Sabine Voelker was most decorated among the women with three medals, silvers at 1,000 and 1,500 meters and a 500 bronze, but the women's speed queen was Sabine's teammate Claudia Pechstein, who won at 3,000 and 5,000 meters. With the latter, she joined Bonnie Blair as the only skaters to win at the same distance in three consecutive Olympics. Yet another German, Anni Friesinger, won gold at 1,500 meters, a popular win not only among the spectators in Salt Lake but also among the 4,500 people in Friesinger's Bavarian home town of Inzell, who were promised free beer if she got gold. A round for the town.

The United States had its finest speedskating performance ever, with six Americans medaling eight times. Chris Witty, a summer-winter Olympian who competed in cycling in Sydney, won gold at 1,000 meters after battling back from mononucleosis, while on the men's side, there was Parra's gold at 1,500 meters and another gold from Casey FitzRandolph at 500 meters. Jennifer Rodriguez of Miami—like Parra a converted in-line skater—won two medals, both bronze.

SHORT TRACK

He wasn't the four-time gold medal winner some people were predicting, but 19-year-old Apolo Anton Ohno of Seattle nonetheless brought short track speedskating into the main room by what he did, and didn't do, at the Salt Lake Ice Center.

In a topsy-turvy four days of competition appropriate for the crash-a-second sport, Ohno had a knack for being in the middle of just about everything. He won two medals, a silver at 1,000 meters when he was lead-

CHUCK WING

CHUCK WING

ing before becoming part of a controversial three-man crash meters from the finish line, and a gold at 1,500 meters when he finished second but was named the winner after Korean Kim Dong-Sung was disqualified for obstruction. Ohno's graciousness at accepting the judge's decisions made him a fan favorite and his phrase "That's short track" became the motto for his sport.

Australia's Steven Bradbury, skating so far in last place that he avoided the collision, crossed the finish line first in the 1,000-meter men's final, a look of disbelief on his face as he realized he'd won gold—the first for an Australian in any winter sport.

Most decorated were Canada's Marc Gagnon, who collected two men's gold medals, and China's Yang Yang (A), who won the first gold medal for China in a Winter Games... and then won China's second. Another Chinese skater named Yang Yang also competed, requiring the (A) for the gold medalist while her teammate was designated with an (S).

That might have seemed odd anywhere else, but in short track it just seemed to fit in with the scenery.

SCOTT G. WINTERTON

Opposite: *One fatal slip takes out Ohno, Ahn and Turcotte on the final turn of the men's 1,000-meter short track race.*

Top: *A crash took out gold-medal hopes for USA's Apolo Ohno, right, along with Hyun-Soo Ahn of Korea and Mathieu Turcotte of Canada.*

Far right: *And the winner is Australia's Steven Bradbury, who missed the pileup but not the finish line for the gold.*

Right: *A fan from the Netherlands sports a large hat with the names of the country's medal winners.*

Above: *Claudia Pechstein of Germany gets a hug from her coach, Joachim Franke, after winning the gold in the women's 5,000-meter event.*

SCOTT G. WINTERTON

CHUCK WING

83

SPEEDSKATING

STUART JOHNSON

Above: *Dong-Sung Kim of Korea drops his flag in disgust after learning he was disqualified for cross-tracking in front of Apolo Ohno of the U.S. in the men's 1,500-meter short-track event.*

Right: *Jochem Uytdehaage of the Netherlands is all smiles after setting a world record in the men's 5,000-meter skate at the Kearns Oval and winning the gold medal.*

Far right: *Catriona Lemay Doan of Canada waves the flag proudly after winning gold in the women's 500-meter skate.*

Opposite: *Germany's Anni Friesinger concentrates as she rounds the track en route to a new world record and a gold medal in the women's 1,500-meter event.*

SCOTT G. WINTERTON

SCOTT G. WINTERTON

SCOTT G. WINTERTON

85

SCOTT G. WINTERTON

SCOTT G. WINTERTON

SCOTT G. WINTERTON

SCOTT G. WINTERTON

Left: *Chris Witty of the United States keeps her eyes on the track as she rounds the turn and heads for a world record in the women's 1,000-meter race at the Olympic Oval.*

Top: *Witty gets a hug and congratulations from her coach, Bart Schouten, after crossing the finish line in world-record time.*

Above left: *Casey FitzRandolph holds the American flag high during a victory lap after winning the men's 500-meter event.*

Above right: *Derek Parra of the United States kneels on the podium after it is announced to the crowd that he is the Olympic champion.*

SCOTT G. WINTERTON

STUART JOHNSON

Top left: *Catriona Lemay Doan of Canada rounds the turn and heads for the finish in the women's 500-meter race at the Kearns Oval.*

Left: *Apolo Anton Ohno of the U.S. raises his hands in victory after receiving his gold medal for winning the men's 1,500-meter race.*

Bottom left: *Germany's Claudia Pechstein raises her arms to celebrate winning the women's 5,000-meter race in world record time.*

Bottom right: *Ohno (369) makes contact with Japan's Satoru Terao and is disqualified for impeding in the 500-meter event.*

SCOTT G. WINTERTON

LAURA SEITZ

87

SCOTT G. WINTERTON

JASON OLSON

CHUCK WING

SCOTT G. WINTERTON

Opposite: *Speed skater Chris Witty of the U.S. holds the American flag as she skates a victory lap after setting a new world record in the women's 1,000-meter event.*

Far left: *China's Yang Yang (A) lets her emotions flow after winning the gold medal in the women's 500-meter short track.*

Above: *Canada's Marc Gagnon, left, sheds tears of joy after he won the gold and his teammate, Jonathan Guilmette, won the silver in the men's 500-meter short track.*

Left: *Krisztina Egyed of Hungary skates like a butterfly during first-day action in the women's 500-meter race at the Olympic Oval.*

89

JEFFREY D. ALLRED

LAURA SEITZ

JEFFREY D. ALLRED

Opposite: Spectators stand trackside and watch during the women's luge at Utah Olympic Park.

Left: Jim Shea of the United States gives thumbs-up to fans after winning gold in the skeleton.

Above: USA-1 driver Todd Hays knows his team put in a silver-medal run in four-man bobsled.

CHAPTER

Eleven

SLIDING SPORTS

HE HAD A PICTURE of a golden-beaked eagle on his helmet, a picture of his gold-medal winning granddad inside the helmet, and under the rails of his skeleton sled, a gold-medal winning run.

Sydney 2000 had its Cathy Freeman. Salt Lake 2002 had its Jim Shea.

Like Freeman, the Aboriginal woman whose 400-meter win on the running track in Sydney galvanized Australia and gave those Games their signature story, Shea's triumph in men's skeleton—first time on the Olympic program in 54 years—stopped America in its tracks, so to speak, and gave the Salt Lake Games its signature story.

The son of a winter Olympian who competed in nordic combined in the 1964 Innsbruck Games and the grandson of a winter Olympian who competed in speedskating, and won two gold medals, in the 1932 Lake Placid Games, 33-year-old Jim Shea was America's first three-generation Olympian. That in itself was a singular accomplishment that prompted the Salt Lake Organizing Committee to invite the three Sheas—Jack, James and Jim—to participate in the opening ceremony as torchbearers. Then, less than three weeks before the Games, Jack Shea, age 91, was killed in an automobile accident in New York. James and Jim still carried the Olympic torch in the opening ceremony and Jim, elected by his U.S. teammates, recited the Athlete's

JOHANNA WORKMAN

Oath, just as Jack had done 70 years ago in Lake Placid. But there was a void with Jack not there, with James and Jim left only to carry him in their hearts.

After the opening ceremony, Jim had to wait nearly two weeks until the skeleton competition at Utah Olympic Park the morning of Feb. 20. The field was a quick one, with former world champion Swissman Gregor Staehli out of retirement just for the Olympics and Austrian Martin Rettl at the top of his game. But there was no denying Jim Shea, who took the lead with the fastest first run and then held on with the second fastest time of the second run to edge Rettl by five-hundredths of a second and Staehli by two-tenths of a second to win gold just like his granddad.

Celebrating with his father at the finish, Jim held up the picture of his grandfather he'd kept stuffed in his helmet. "He had some unfinished business before he went to heaven," said Jim, pointing to the photo. "Now I think he can go on."

As good as the Jim Shea story was, it was far from the only show-stopping tale that took place during 15 days of nonstop sliding at the Olympic Park track. Virtually every day, someone was doing something extraordinary, outstanding and often totally unexpected.

In women's skeleton, Tristan Gale, New Mexican-born and transplanted to Salt Lake because of the Olympic track, and U.S. teammate Lea Ann Parsley, an Ohio firefighter, won gold-silver to give Shea plenty of USA company on the winner's podium.

In bobsled, America also shined, winning the country's first bob medals since 1956. Home course advantage indeed. Driver Todd Hays and his team of Randy Jones, Bill Schuffenhauer and Garrett Hines took silver in the four-man competition, just ahead of driver Brian Shimer and his team of Mike Kohn, Doug Sharp and Dan Steele. For both Hayes, 33, and Shimer, 39, the medals represented decades of work without podium results. Hays competed in Nagano in 1998 but did not place among the top eight and Shimer had competed on four previous Olympic teams, from Calgary on. His previous bests had been a seventh in two-man in 1992 and a fifth in four-man in 1998.

The shock of the Games was reserved for the women's two-person race—the first women's bobsled competition in Olympic history. The American team of Jill Bakken and Vonetta Flowers took gold to the surprise of everyone. The favored American team of Jean Racine and Gea Johnson faded to fifth place after a pre-race injury to Johnson limited her pushing ability at the start.

German teams took bronze in the women's bobsled competition and gold in the four-man, but it was in luge that the Germans really loaded up. Germany's Sylke Otto won women's luge singles, the team of Patric-Fritz Leitner and Alexander Resch won doubles and in an upset, German luge legend Georg Hackl, winner of the last three Olympics men's singles, took silver behind Italy's Armin Zoggeler, who placed third to Hackl in 1994 and second in 1998. The American teams of Mark Grimmette-Brian Martin and Chris Thorpe-Clay Ives finished silver-bronze in doubles. With partner Gordon Sheer, Thorpe had taken silver in Nagano, while Grimmette and Martin moved up a spot from their bronze medal finish in the Nagano Games.

SLIDING SPORTS

JEFFREY D. ALLRED

JASON OLSON

JOHANNA WORKMAN

LAURA SEITZ

Opposite: *The USA team of Jill Bakken and Vonetta Flowers take a perfect line for a gold-medal run.*

Above: *Jim Shea is all concentration as he heads down the track for a gold in the skeleton.*

Top right: *The USA-1 team gets a perfect start for the third run of the four-man bobsled event.*

Right: *Pete Later, Kyle Perry, Matt Dolan and Johnny Evanson braved the cold and bad makeup to cheer on the USA.*

Bottom far right: *Flowers wipes away tears having realized she and Bakken have won the gold in women's bobsled.*

JEFFREY D. ALLRED

Far left: *Jim Shea gives a yell after receiving his gold medal in men's skeleton.*

Left: *Americans Mark Grimmette and Brian Martin react after being bumped down to a silver medal.*

Below: *The USA-2 team is a blur as it launches for its fourth and final run in the four-man bobsled at Utah Olympic Park.*

JASON OLSON

JASON OLSON

SLIDING SPORTS

JEFFREY D. ALLRED

JEFFREY D. ALLRED

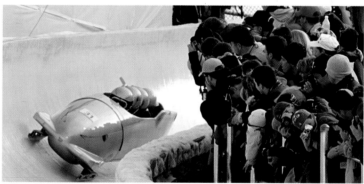

JASON OLSON

LAURA SEITZ

Far left: *Germany's Patric-Fritz Leitner and Alexander Besch hear that they have won the gold in two-man luge.*

Top: *The USA-2 team celebrate the winning of the bronze medal in the four-man bobsled.*

Above: *The four-man team from the Virgin Islands makes its way down the track on its first run.*

Left: *Austria's Martin Rettl gets into the mood of the Games in a very colorful way.*

95

JEFFREY D. ALLRED

JEFFREY D. ALLRED

JEFFREY D. ALLRED

JEFFREY D. ALLRED

Far left: Jim Shea holds a picture of his grandfather in his right hand as he reacts to the crowd after his winning run.

Above: The Germany 2 team reacts to news that it won a gold medal in the four-man bobsled.

Left: Italy's Armin Zoeggeler reacts after learning he won a gold in the luge.

Opposite: Vonetta Flowers sheds tears of joy as she receives her medal along with her teammate, Jill Bakken, of the USA.

JASON OLSON

97

SLIDING SPORTS

JEFFREY D. ALLRED

JEFFREY D. ALLRED

JEFFREY D. ALLRED

JASON OLSON

Top left: *Germany's Barbara Niederhuber (8), Sylke Otto and Silke Kraushaar made a clean sweep of the medals in women's luge.*

Far left: *Sylke Otto knows she put down a winning run as she coasts to a stop on her gold medal sled.*

Left: *The USA-2 team learns that it was fast enough to win a bronze in the four-man bobsled at the Utah Olympic Park.*

Above: *Tristan Gale of the United States finds out just how heavy a gold medal can be after her win in the women's skeleton.*

LAURA SEITZ

JASON OLSON

JASON OLSON

Left: *Tristan Gale, left, and Lea Ann Parsley can't quit smiling as they wait for the awarding of their medals.*

Top: *It was Gale, right, winning the gold and Parsley winning the silver in the women's skeleton competition.*

Above *Fans standing trackside hold out their hands to congratulate Gale on her medal-winning run in the skeleton at the Utah Olympic Park.*

99

LAURA SEITZ

RAVELL CALL

Opposite: *Norway's skip Paal Trulsen throws the final stone for his team in the gold medal match against Canada. The Norwegians prevailed by a single point.*

Above: *The housewives from Scotland parade on the victory stand wearing their curling gold medals as jewelry.*

Right: *After breaking a 3–3 tie with the last stone of the match, Great Britain team members celebrate their championship as the silver-medal winning Swiss look on.*

JASON OLSON

CHAPTER
Twelve
CURLING

JOKES AND SNICKERS ASIDE, no sport in the Salt Lake Olympics gained more respect than curling. With its curious blend of ice, stones, brooms and a scoring area called the house, and with few understanding the game, curling was the brunt of most pre-Olympic jokes. But with NBC and its various cable entities broadcasting entire curling matches from the Ogden Ice Sheet, interest surely and not all that slowly picked up. By the end of the two-week tournament, the Ice Sheet was regularly sold out with people waiting outside to pick up a spare ticket. Even ticket scalpers embraced curling.

What curling lacks in action it makes up for in suspense. No more was that obvious than when Norway upset the favorites, Canada, 6–5 for the men's gold and Great Britain, utilizing four housewives from Scotland, armed with brooms and cooking-pot-shaped stones, beat Switzerland, 4–3.

In a pleasant surprise for a country just beginning to understand curling, the American women missed out on a bronze, falling to Canada, 9–5.

Spectators discovered that curling, said to have found its roots in Scotland in the 16th century, is actually a game of chess played on an ice-covered bowling alley. And, as with any of the Olympic sports, it is a game of inches.

The most stunning upset came in men's gold-medal play. With the score tied 5–5 and Canada's captain, Kevin Martin, the Tiger Woods of a game second only to hockey among his countrymen, making the final throw, it was, by all rights, a gimme.

Instead, the stone barely slid past its target. "It was a little deep," explained Martin, "about an inch." Norway got the point and the title.

In the game for the men's bronze, Switzerland beat Sweden, 7–3.

The outstanding play by the Scottish housewives took curling from late-night to prime-time viewing in England, with break-in live reports. Britain's last gold

medal in the Winter Olympics came in 1984 by ice dancers Jayne Torville and Christopher Dean. Since then, Britain's most publicized performance was that of fledgling ski jumper Eddie Edwards, aka Eddie the Eagle, in 1988.

The Brits beat the Swiss by a single point earned in the 10th and final end.

The Americans were encouraged by their higher-than-expected 4th-place finish, but happier that their sport finally got some respect. "I just hope that the word gets out, that people learn about our sport instead of making fun of it," said U.S. team member Debbie McCormick. "If people would just watch it or try it," added teammate Ann Swisshelm, "they'll love it."

JASON OLSON

LAURA SEITZ

LAURA SEITZ

LAURA SEITZ

CURLING

XIX OLYMPIC WINTER GAMES

LAURA SEITZ

Opposite left: *Team Switzerland celebrates winning the men's bronze curling medal with a win over Sweden at the Ice Sheet.*

Opposite top: *Janice Rankin and Fiona MacDonald work the ice in advance of the stone.*

Opposite middle: *Canada skip Kevin Martin, left, braces himself after Canada loses gold to Norway. Flemming Davanger of Team Norway exults over the win.*

Opposite bottom: *Sweden skip Peja Lindholm concedes the bronze medal game against Switzerland by jokingly going fast past the hog line and placing the stone in the button.*

Top: *Silver, gold and bronze men's curling teams from Canada, left, Norway and Switzerland salute the crowd.*

Right: *Great Britain's Debbie Knox yells instructions to her sweepers during the women's gold medal match against Switzerland.*

Far right: *U.S. curler Ann Swisshelm shoots the stone as Stacey Liapis, left front, and Debbie McCormick get set to sweep.*

JASON OLSON

RAVELL CALL

103

RAVELL CALL

JOHANNA WORKMAN

Opposite: The day before the Olympics began, the Medals Plaza, in the foreground, was a quiet place for a stroll. That would soon change.

Above: Children with lanterns perform on the Medals Plaza stage the evening of Feb. 18.

Far right: Ed Robertson of Barenaked Ladies shows his Canadian roots while headlining a Medals Plaza concert.

Right: John Rzezenik, lead singer of the Goo Goo Dolls, plays rock guitar and sings at the Medals Plaza.

CHUCK WING

LAURA SEITZ

CHAPTER
Thirteen
OLYMPIC SCENES

FOR 17 DAYS they were jammed with people from all places and all walks of life, but with a single purpose: to be a part of the Olympic experience.

Salt Lake's streets had never seen anything like it and may never see anything like it again. In unprecedented numbers they came, disembarking from trains, cars, buses and taxi cabs, some pushing baby carriages, some pushing themselves in wheelchairs, some carrying pockets full of pins to trade, others carrying signs that said "I Need 1," still others carrying signs that said "Free Tibet."

On all three Saturday nights of the Olympic period—Feb. 9, 16 and 23—Olympic Square, where the Ice Center and Medal's Plaza were situated, was shut off to all but event ticket-holders. There were simply too many people. Downtown closed!

But Olympic Square always reopened, and the people never stopped coming and going. From the Gallivan Center, where Bud World set up shop, to Temple Square, from Washington Square to the new Gateway and its Olympic Plaza, an Olympisized Salt Lake City, its buildings wrapped in Olympians, literally welcomed the world.

105

KEVIN LEE

PAUL BARKER

KEVIN LEE

PETER CHUDLEIGH

Top: *Speedskating star Jochem Uytdehaage gets gold medal treatment at the Heineken House.*

Above: *A world globe at the center of the Gallivan Center welcomes the world.*

Right: *Marty and Rene Furmanski, left foreground, were among 10 couples who renewed their vows on Valentines Day at the Coca-Cola Pin Trading Center.*

Far right: *High above it all, the Olympic flame burns bright in its caldron on the south side of Rice-Eccles Olympic Stadium.*

KEVIN LEE

KEVIN LEE

KEVIN LEE

Top: *Utah Governor Mike Leavitt, left, applauds as former New York City Mayor Rudy Giuliani addresses a gathering at the Utah Museum of Fine Arts. Giuliani attended closing ceremonies.*

Above: *A fire-thrower appears to be challenging a Paralympic skier. It was all part of the nightly atmosphere on Olympic Square.*

Right: *Park City's Main Street was closed to traffic during the Olympic period. At least to the kind with four wheels.*

107

JOHANNA WORKMAN

JOHANNA WORKMAN

JEFFREY D. ALLRED

Far left: *Nelly Furtado gives the crowd some mike time during her performance at the Medals Plaza the evening of February 18.*

Above: *At Soldier Hollow, SLOC President Mitt Romney thanks Norwegian fans for coming out, and the feeling appears to be mutual.*

Left: *See Spot jump through the five rings.*

Opposite: *A huge hockey puck bounces its way above a huge crowd the night of February 19 at the Medals Plaza.*

STUART JOHNSON

SCOTT G. WINTERTON

KEVIN LEE

MICHAEL BRANDY

STUART JOHNSON

KEVIN LEE

Opposite: For 17 days, the Olympic flame at the Medals Plaza kept downtown Salt Lake hot.

Top left: Surreal animals make their way through Olympic Square.

Above: 1952 double gold medalist skier Andrea Mead Lawrence holds her award as "No. 1 Greatest Winter Olympian" as voted by Olympic filmmaker Bud Greenspan, left.

Far left: As the Games end, souvenir-toting soldiers board a plane for home.

Left: A pin trader sets up on a downtown sidewalk and quickly attracts a crowd.

111

TOM SMART

JEFFREY D. ALLRED

TOM SMART

TOM SMART

RAVELL CALL

Top left: *Former Super Bowl-winning quarterback and 2002 lead volunteer Steve Young was the headliner who announced the nightly headliners at the Medals Plaza.*

Above: *On the eve of the Games, an estimated 50,000 people flock to the City & County Building and surrounding Washington Square to greet the Olympic flame.*

Middle left: *With sunrise hurrying to catch up, spectators make their way to the luge finals Feb. 11 at Utah Olympic Park.*

Bottom left: *Maybe every Olympic spectator won't remember every single detail. It's why you take photographs.*

Left: *Alanis Morissette and friends.*

Opposite: *Navajo artisan Nanabe Aragon weaves a rug at the Discover Navajo 2002 exhibit at the Gateway Center.*

TOM SMART

113

STUART JOHNSON

Left: *At Soldier Hollow, a western experience complete with cowboys around a campfire entertains spectators on their way to cross country racing.*

Bottom left: *Joyce Morgan and Brenda Larsen are all smiles as they wear their roots USA berets after waiting in line to buy the hats made enormously popular by the Games.*

Below: *For 17 days the Gallivan Center in downtown Salt Lake is transformed into Bud World.*

Bottom: *The crowd goes wild at Heineken House in downtown Salt Lake at news of more speedskating gold for the Dutch.*

Opposite: *From medal to metal: Canadian pairs skaters David Pelletier and Jamie Sale rock with Barenaked Ladies.*

KEVIN LEE

PETER CHUDLEIGH

KEVIN LEE

LAURA SEITZ

PETER CHUDLEIGH

JOHANNA WORKMAN

CHAPTER
Fourteen
CLOSING CEREMONY

Opposite: *Olympic Stadium is ablaze in the spectacular fireworks show that closed the Games.*

Above: *Salt Lake Mayor Rocky Anderson, left, and IOC President Jacques Rogge applaud after Rocky transfers Olympic flag to the mayor of Torino, Italy, Sergio Chiamparino.*

Right: *Swirling skaters perform during the pomp and ceremony of closing ceremonies.*

JOHANNA WORKMAN

A T 8:34 P.M. ON FEB. 24, 2002, the first groans of protest were heard in Rice-Eccles Olympic Stadium.

The flame in the Olympic caldron was extinguished.

Moments before that, the lights were turned off on the five interlocking rings in the foothills.

Salt Lake City's 17 days of glory were over.

The curtain came down as part of an emotional closing ceremony that featured music, tributes and, at the end, the largest fireworks display in western history as fireworks were launched simultaneously from 11 different stations along the Wasatch Range.

Speaking to the athletes of the 2002 Winter Games as a crowd that included vice president Dick Cheney listened, Salt Lake Organizing Committee President Mitt Romney said, "Olympians, we cheered all of you, not just our own. We saw in you the universal greatness of the human family. During these Games of 2002 in Salt Lake you have shown us what the world can be."

Then Romney added, "In a few moments we will extinguish the Olympic flame, but the fire you have lit in each of us will not go out. We leave this place as dreamers because now we know that the dream we share can come true. Olympians, volunteers, spectators, remember these 17 days; we have rocked the world!"

IOC President Jacques Rogge then took the mike and said, "People of America, Utah, and Salt Lake City, you have given the world superb Games. You have reassured us that people from all countries can live peacefully together."

"I now declare the XIX Olympic Winter Games closed, and in accordance with tradition I call upon the youth of the world to assemble four years from now in Turin to celebrate with us there, the XX Olympic Games."

With that, country music legend Willie Nelson came on stage to sing "Bridge Over Troubled Water" prior to the extinguishing of the flame, the spectacular fireworks show, and a final closing rock concert by Bon Jovi. The Games may have ended, but they did not end quietly.

JOHANNA WORKMAN

JEFFREY D. ALLRED

JOHANNA WORKMAN

Top: Dance skating team Renee Roca and Gorsha Sur grace the ice just before the caldron is extinguished.

Above: Huge white flags lap the ice as a slide show of Olympic proportion uses them as a screen..

Left: Skeleton gold medalist Jim Shea of Team USA is carried on the shoulders of athletes from many nations as the 2002 Olympians move onto the Olympic Stadium floor.

JEREMY HARMON

JEFFREY D. ALLRED

JOHANNA WORKMAN

Far left: *Fireworks erupt above the Olympic rings in the Salt Lake foothills as the Games of Salt Lake draw to a close.*

Above: *Showing his colors: legendary rock star Jon Bon Jovi takes the Olympic Stadium stage wrapped in America's best.*

Left: *Ilia Kulik, men's gold medalist figure skater in Nagano, spins on the ice during the Big Band entertainment portion of the closing ceremony.*

119

JOHANNA WORKMAN

JOHANNA WORKMAN

JEFFREY D. ALLRED

Far left: *Suspended on necks 25 meters high, dinosaurs make an appearance at the closing ceremony. Dystophaeus and Allosaurus are meant to represent Utah's "first family." Their closing ceremony "voices" belong to Donny and Marie Osmond.*

Above: *Five lighted balloons rise 100 feet above the floor of the stadium as the Children of Light file into the stadium to say thank you to the athletes for extraordinary competition and inspiration.*

Left: *KISS brings its trademark makeup and music to the Games.*

JOHANNA WORKMAN

JOHANNA WORKMAN

Top: *Olympian Scott Hamilton leaps in the air as the Children of Light pass before him.*

Above:. *Italy's national flag-spinning team performs while representing the regions of Italy that will host the 2006 Olympic Winter Games in Torino.*

Right: *A skater splashes ultraviolet paint to create a spectacular multi-colored palette on the stadium floor.*

LAURA SEITZ

TOM SMART

JOHANNA WORKMAN

JOHANNA WORKMAN

Above: *From stations all along the eastern bench, fireworks explode at the conclusion of closing ceremonies, illuminating Olympic City one last time.*

Far left: *Ice dancers perform prior to the extinguishing of the flame.*

Left: *Flags carried by skaters circle the ice in preparation of the flag slide show.*

122

STUART JOHNSON

JEFFREY D.ALLRED

Far Left: *The Olympic flag is transported out of the stadium by The Child of Light (Utahn Ryne Sanborn).*

Left: *As athletes from the world listen, surprise performer Willie Nelson sings "Bridge Over Troubled Water."*

Below: *After the flame is extinguished, the Olympic caldron remains in the spotlight.*

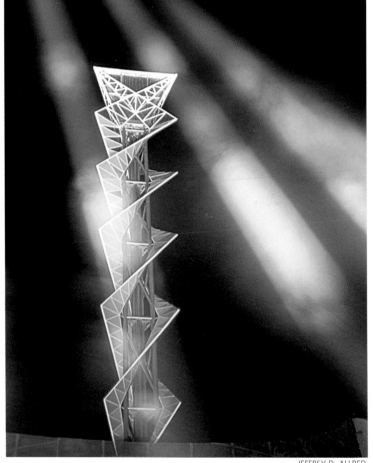

JEFFREY D. ALLRED

123

JEFFREY D. ALLRED

MEDAL Results
2002 • SALT LAKE CITY

ALPINE SKIING

Men's downhill
(At Snowbasin Ski Area)

GOLD: Fritz Strobl, Austria
SILVER: Lasse Kjus, Norway
BRONZE: Stephan Eberharter, Austria

Women's downhill
(At Snowbasin Ski Area)

GOLD: Carole Montillet, France
SILVER: Isolde Kostner, Italy
BRONZE: Renate Goetschl, Austria

Men's alpine combined
(At Snowbasin Ski Area)

GOLD: Kjetil Andre Aamodt, Norway
SILVER: Bode Miller, USA
BRONZE: Benjamin Raich, Austria

Women's alpine combined
(At Snowbasin Ski Area)

GOLD: Janica Kostelic, Croatia
SILVER: Renate Goetschl, Austria
BRONZE: Martina Ertl, Germany

Men's super-G
(At Snowbasin Ski Area)

GOLD: Kjetil Andre Aamodt, Norway
SILVER: Stephan Eberharter, Austria
BRONZE: Andreas Schifferer, Austria

Women's super-G
(At Snowbasin Ski Area)

GOLD: Daniela Ceccarelli, Italy
SILVER: Janica Kostelic, Croatia
BRONZE: Karen Putzer, Italy

David Pelletier and Jamie Sale—
Gold Medals, Figure Skating Pairs

Men's slalom
(At Deer Valley Resort)

GOLD: Jean-Pierre Vidal, France
SILVER: Sebastien Amiez, France
BRONZE: Alain Baxter, Gr. Britain

*As of 4/6/02 the awarding of the bronze medal is under investigation.

Women's slalom
(At Deer Valley Resort)

GOLD: Janica Kostelic, Croatia
SILVER: Laure Pequegnot, France
BRONZE: Anja Paerson, Sweden

Men's giant slalom
(At Park City Mountain Resort)

GOLD: Stephan Eberharter, Austria
SILVER: Bode Miller, USA
BRONZE: Lasse Kjus, Norway

Women's giant slalom
(At Deer Valley Resort)

GOLD: Janica Kostelic, Croatia
SILVER: Anja Paerson, Sweden
BRONZE: Sonja Nef, Switzerland

BIATHLON
(At Soldier Hollow)

Men's 20-kilometer individual

GOLD: Ole Einar Bjoerndalen, Nor.
SILVER: Frank Luck, Germany
BRONZE: Victor Maigourov, Russia

Women's 15-kilometer individual

GOLD: Andrea Henkel, Germany
SILVER: Liv Grete Poiree, Norway
BRONZE: Magdalena Forsberg, Sweden

Men's 10-kilometer sprint

GOLD: Ole Einar Bjoerndalen, Nor.
SILVER: Sven Fischer, Germany
BRONZE: Wolfgang Perner, Austria

Women's 7.5-kilometer sprint

GOLD: Kati Wilhelm, Germany
SILVER: Uschi Disl, Germany
BRONZE: Magdalena Forsberg, Sweden

Men's 12.5-kilometer pursuit

GOLD: Ole Einar Bjoerndalen, Norway
SILVER: Raphael Poiree, France
BRONZE: Ricco Gross, Germany

Women's 10-kilometer pursuit

GOLD: Olga Pyleva, Russia
SILVER: Kati Wilhelm, Germany
BRONZE: Irina Nikoultchina, Bulgaria

Women's 4x7.5-kilometer relay

GOLD: Germany (Apel, Henkel, Disl, Wilhelm)
SILVER: Norway (Andreassen, Poiree, Skjelbreid, Tjoerhom)
BRONZE: Russia (Pyleva, Koukleva, Ishmouratova, Akhatova)

Men's 4x7.5-kilometer relay

GOLD: Norway (Andresen, Bjoerndalen, Gjelland, Hanevold)
SILVER: Germany (Fischer, Luck, Sendell, Gross)
BRONZE: France (Defrasne, Marguet, Poiree, Robert)

BOBSLED
(At Utah Olympic Park)

Men's two-man

GOLD: Germany 1 (Christoph Langen & Markus Zimmermann)
SILVER: Switzerland 1 (Christian Reich & Steve Anderhub)
BRONZE: Switzerland 2 (Martin Annen & Beat Heft)
TRACK RECORD: 47.44 seconds, Langen, Germany (third run)

Women's two-woman

GOLD: USA 2 (Jill Bakken & Vonetta Flowers)
SILVER: Germany 1 (Sandra Prokoff & Ulrike Holzner)
BRONZE: Germany 2 (Susi-Lisa Erdmann & Nicole Herschmann)
TRACK RECORD: 48.51 seconds, Bakken, USA (first run)

Tristan Gale—Gold Medal, Skeleton

Men's four-man

GOLD: Germany 2 (Lange, Kuehn, Kuske, Embach)
SILVER: USA 1 (Hays, Jones, Schuffenhauer, Hines)
BRONZE: USA 2 (Shimer, Kohn, Sharp, Steele)

CROSS COUNTRY
(At Soldier Hollow)

Women's 15-kilometer freestyle

GOLD: Stefania Belmondo, Italy
SILVER: Larissa Lazutina, Russia
BRONZE: Katerina Neumannova, Czech Republic

Men's 30-kilometer freestyle

GOLD: Johann Muehlegg, Spain
SILVER: Christian Hoffmann, Austria
BRONZE: Mikhail Botvinov, Austria

Women's 10-kilometer classical

GOLD: Bente Skari, Norway
SILVER: Olga Danilova, Russia
BRONZE: Julija Tchepalova, Russia

Men's 15-kilometer classical

GOLD: Andrus Veerpalu, Estonia
SILVER: Frode Estil, Norway
BRONZE: Jaak Mae, Estonia

Men's 10K+ pursuit

GOLD: Johann Muehlegg, Spain
SILVER: Frode Estil, Norway
SILVER: Thomas Alsgaard, Norway

Women's 5K+ pursuit

GOLD: Olga Danilova, Russia
SILVER: Larissa Lazutina, Russia
BRONZE: Beckie Scott, Canada

Men's 4x10-kilometer relay

GOLD: Norway (Aukland, Estil, Skjeldal, Alsgaard)
SILVER: Italy (Jaj, di Centa, Piller Cottrer, Zorzi)
BRONZE: Germany (Filbrich, Schluetter, Angerer, Sommerfeldt)

Women's 1.5-kilometer sprint

GOLD: Julija Tchepalova, Russia
SILVER: Evi Sachenbacher, Germany
BRONZE: Anita Moen, Norway

Men's 1.5-kilometer sprint

GOLD: Tore Arne Hetland, Norway
SILVER: Peter Schlickenrieder, Germany
BRONZE: Christian Zorzi, Italy

Women's 4x5-kilometer relay

GOLD: Germany (Henkel, Bauer, Kuenzel, Sachenbacher)
SILVER: Norway (Bjoergen, Skari, Pedersen, Moen)
BRONZE: Switzerland (Huber, Rochat, Albrecht Loretan, Leonardi Cortesi)

Men's 50-kilometer classical

GOLD: Mikhail Ivanov, Russia
SILVER: Andrus Veerpalu, Estonia
BRONZE: Odd-Bjoern Hjelmeset, Norway

*Spain's Johann Muelegg was stripped of the gold for testing positive for a performance-enhancing drug.

Women's 30-kilometer classical

GOLD: Gabriella Paruzzi, Italy
SILVER: Stefania Belmondo, Italy
BRONZE: Bente Skari, Norway

* Russia's Larissa Lazutina was stripped of the gold for testing positive for a performance-enhancing drug.

CURLING
(At the Ice Sheet at Ogden)

Women's tournament

GOLD: Great Britain (Knox, MacDonald, Martin, Morton, Rankin)
SILVER: Switzerland (Bidaud, Ebnoether, Frei, Ott, Roethlisberger)
BRONZE: Canada (Law, Nelson, Noble, Skinner, Wheatcroft)

Jim Shea—Gold Medal, Skeleton

Men's tournament

GOLD: Norway (Trulsen, Vaagberg, Davanger, Ramsfjell, Nergaard)
SILVER: Canada (Martin, Walchuck, Rycroft, Bartlett, Tralnberg)
BRONZE: Switzerland (A. Schwaller, C. Schwaller, Eggler, Crichting, Ramstein)

FIGURE SKATING
(At the Salt Lake Ice Center)

Pairs

GOLD: Elena Berezhnaya & Anton Sikharulidze, Russia
GOLD: Jamie Sale & David Pelletier, Canada
BRONZE: Xue Shen & Hongbo Zhao, China

Men's singles

GOLD: Alexei Yagudin, Russia
SILVER: Evgeni Plushenko, Russia
BRONZE: Timothy Goebel, USA

Ice dancing

GOLD: Marina Anissina & Gwendal Peizerat, France
SILVER: Irina Lobacheva & Ilia Averbukh, Russia
BRONZE: Barbara Fusar Poli & Maurizio Margaglio, Italy

Ladies singles

GOLD: Sarah Hughes, USA
SILVER: Irina Slutskaya, Russia
BRONZE: Michelle Kwan, USA

FREESTYLE SKIING
(At Deer Valley Resort)

Women's moguls

GOLD: Kari Traa, Norway
SILVER: Shannon Bahrke, USA
BRONZE: Tae Satoya, Japan

Men's moguls

GOLD: Janne Lahtela, Finland
SILVER: Travis Mayer, USA
BRONZE: Richard Gay, France

Women's aerials

GOLD: Alisa Camplin, Australia
SILVER: Veronica Brenner, Canada
BRONZE: Deidra Dionne, Canada

Men's aerials

GOLD: Alex Valenta, Czech Republic
SILVER: Joe Pack, USA
BRONZE: Alexei Grichin, Belarus

ICE HOCKEY
(At the E Center & The Peaks Ice Arena)

Women's tournament

GOLD: Canada
SILVER: United States
BRONZE: Sweden

Men's tournament

GOLD: Canada
SILVER: United States
BRONZE: Russia

LUGE
(At Utah Olympic Park)

Men's singles

GOLD: Armin Zoeggeler, Italy
SILVER: Georg Hackl, Germany
BRONZE: Markus Prock, Austria
TRACK RECORD: 44.271, Prock, Austria, Feb. 11, 2002 (third run)

Women's singles

GOLD: Sylke Otto, Germany
SILVER: Barbara Niedernhuber, Germany
BRONZE: Silke Kraushaar, Germany
TRACK RECORD: 42.940, Otto, Germany, Feb. 13, 2002 (third run)

Doubles

GOLD: Patric-Fritz Leitner & Alexander Resch, Germany
SILVER: Brian Martin & Mark Grimmette, USA
BRONZE: Chris Thorpe & Clay Ives, USA
TRACK RECORD: 42.953, Leitner & Resch, Germany, Feb. 15, 2002 (first run)

NORDIC COMBINED
(At Utah Olympic Park & Soldier Hollow)

Individual K90 jumping / 15K skiing

GOLD: Samppa Lajunen, Finland
SILVER: Jaakko Tallus, Finland
BRONZE: Felix Gottwald, Austria

Team K90 jumping / 4x5K relay

GOLD: Finland (Mantila, Manninen, Tallus, Lajunen)
SILVER: Germany (Kircheisen, Hettich, Hoehlig, Ackermann)
BRONZE: Austria (Bieler, Gruber, Stecher, Gottwald)

Individual K120 jumping / 7.5K sprint

GOLD: Samppa Lajunen, Finland
SILVER: Ronny Ackermann, Germany
BRONZE: Felix Gottwald, Austria

SHORT-TRACK SPEEDSKATING
(At the Salt Lake Ice Center)

Women's 1,500 meters

GOLD: Gi-Hyun Ko, Korea
SILVER: Eun-Kyung Choi, Korea
BRONZE: Evgenia Radanova, Bulgaria
WORLD, OLYMPIC RECORDS: Choi, Korea (in semifinals) 2:21.069

Women's 500 meters

GOLD: Yang Yang (A), China
SILVER: Evgenia Radanova, Bulgaria
BRONZE: Chunlu Wang, China
OLYMPIC RECORD: 44.118, Yang (A), China (in semifinals)

Men's 1,000 meters

GOLD: Steven Bradbury, Australia
SILVER: Apolo Anton Ohno, USA
BRONZE: Mathieu Turcotte, Canada
OLYMPIC RECORD: Turcotte, Canada (in quarterfinals) 1:27.185

Women's 3,000-meter relay

GOLD: Korea (M. Choi, Joo, Park, E. Choi)
SILVER: China (Yang (A), Yang (S), Wang, Sun)
BRONZE: Canada (Charest, Drolet, Coulet-Nadon, Kraus, Vicent)
WORLD AND OLYMPIC RECORD: 4:12.793, Korea (in finals)

Joe Pack—Silver Medal, Aerials

Men's 1,500 meters

GOLD: Apolo Anton Ohno, USA
SILVER: Jiajun Li, China
BRONZE: Marc Gagnon, Canada
OLYMPIC RECORD: 2:15.924, Dong-Sung Kim, Korea (in semifinals)

Men's 500 meters

GOLD: Marc Gagnon, Canada
SILVER: Jonathan Guilmette, Canada
BRONZE: Rusty Smith, USA
OLYMPIC RECORD: 41.082, Dong-Sung Kim, Korea (in quarterfinals)

Men's 5,000-meter relay

GOLD: Canada (Turcotte, Tremblay, Gagnon, Guilmette)
SILVER: Italy (Franceschina, Rodigari, Carta, Carnino)
BRONZE: China (Li, Feng, Li, Guo)
OLYMPIC RECORD: 6:45.455, Canada (in preliminaries)

Women's 1,000 meters

GOLD: Yang Yang (A), China
SILVER: Gi-Hyun Ko, Korea
BRONZE: Yang Yang (S), China
OLYMPIC RECORD: 1:31.235, Yang (A), China (in quarterfinals)

SKELETON
(At Utah Olympic Park)

Men's singles

GOLD: Jim Shea Jr., USA
SILVER: Martin Rettl, Austria
BRONZE: Gregor Staehli, Switzerland

Women's singles

GOLD: Tristan Gale, USA
SILVER: Lea Ann Parsley, USA
BRONZE: Alex Coomber, Great Britain

SKI JUMPING
(At Utah Olympic Park)

Individual K90

GOLD: Simon Ammann, Switzerland
SILVER: Sven Hannawald, Germany
BRONZE: Adam Malysz, Poland

Apolo Ohno—Gold Medal, Short-track

Individual K120

GOLD: Simon Ammann, Switzerland
SILVER: Adam Malysz, Poland
BRONZE: Matti Hautamaeki, Finland

Team K120

GOLD: Germany (Hannawald, Hocke, Uhrmann, Schmitt)
SILVER: Finland (Hautamaeki, Lindstroem, Jussilainen, Ahonen)
BRONZE: Slovakia (Fras, Peterka, Kranjec, Zonta)

SNOWBOARDING
(At Park City Mountain Resort)

Women's halfpipe
SUNDAY, FEB. 10

GOLD: Kelly Clark, USA
SILVER: Doriane Vidal, France
BRONZE: Fabienne Reuteler, Switzerland

Men's halfpipe

GOLD: Ross Powers, USA
SILVER: Danny Kass, USA
BRONZE: Jarret Thomas, USA

Men's parallel giant slalom

GOLD: Philipp Schoch, Switzerland
SILVER: Richard Richardsson, Sweden
BRONZE: Chris Klug, USA

Women's parallel giant slalom

GOLD: Isabelle Blanc, France
SILVER: Karine Ruby, France
BRONZE: Lidia Trettel, Italy

SPEEDSKATING
(At Utah Olympic Oval)

Men's 5,000 meters

GOLD: Jochem Uytdehaage, Netherlands
SILVER: Derek Parra, USA
BRONZE: Jens Boden, Germany
WORLD, OLYMPIC RECORDS: 6:14.66, Uytdehaage, Netherlands

Women's 3,000 meters

GOLD: Claudia Pechstein, Germany
SILVER: Renate Groenewold, Netherlands
BRONZE: Cindy Klassen, Canada
WORLD, OLYMPIC RECORDS: 3:57.70, Pechstein, Germany

Men's 500 meters

GOLD: Casey FitzRandolph, USA
SILVER: Hiroyasu Shimizu, Japan
BRONZE: Kip Carpenter, USA
OLYMPIC RECORD: 34.42, FitzRandolph, USA (first day)

Women's 500 meters

GOLD: Catriona Le May Doan, Canada
SILVER: Monique Garbrecht-Enfeldt, Germany
BRONZE: Sabine Voelker, Germany
OLYMPIC RECORD: 37.30, LeMay Doan, Canada (first day)

Men's 1,000 meters

GOLD: Gerard van Velde, Netherlands
SILVER: Jan Bos, Netherlands
BRONZE: Joey Cheek, USA
WORLD, OLYMPIC RECORDS: 1:07.18, van Velde, Netherlands

Women's 1,000 meters
SUNDAY, FEB. 17

GOLD: Chris Witty, USA
SILVER: Sabine Voelker, Germany

BRONZE: Jennifer Rodriguez, USA
WORLD, OLYMPIC RECORDS: 1:13.83, Witty, USA

Men's 1,500 meters

GOLD: Derek Parra, USA
SILVER: Jochem Uytdehaage, Netherlands
BRONZE: Adne Sondral, Norway

WORLD, OLYMPIC RECORDS: 1:43.95, Parra, USA

Women's 1,500 meters

GOLD: Anni Friesinger, Germany
SILVER: Sabine Voelker, Germany
BRONZE: Jennifer Rodriguez, USA
WORLD, OLYMPIC RECORDS: Friesinger, Germany, 1:54.02

Medal count by country

	GOLD	SILVER	BRONZE	TOTAL
Germany	12	16	7	35
United States	10	13	11	34
Norway	11	7	6	24
Canada	6	3	8	17
Russia	6	6	4	16
Austria	2	4	10	16
Italy	4	4	4	12
France	4	5	2	11
Switzerland	3	2	6	11
Netherlands	3	5	0	8
China	2	2	4	8
Finland	4	2	1	7
Sweden	0	2	4	6

	GOLD	SILVER	BRONZE	TOTAL
Croatia	3	1	0	4
Korea	2	2	0	4
Estonia	1	1	1	3
Britain	1	0	2	3
Bulgaria	0	1	2	3
Australia	2	0	0	2
Spain	2	0	0	2
Czech Republic	1	0	1	2
Japan	0	1	1	2
Poland	0	1	1	2
Belarus	0	0	1	1
Slovenia	0	0	1	1

127

Letter from the Deseret News editor

Dear Reader:

It is a rare and wonderful opportunity when the world's biggest sporting event and multinational gathering happens in your home town. For 17 days as the XIX Olympic Winter Games took place in our home town, the Deseret News was there, covering the spectacle from every possible angle and with every available resource.

From our photographers and reporters on the front lines to our editors and paginators huddled in the office, collecting, editing and producing, the process ran almost literally around the clock.

Yes, it was exhausting but more than that it was exhilarating and satisfying being the "paper of record" while chronicling memories for the world.

In these pages, we have reproduced photographs and retold many of the memorable stories of the Games of 2002. It was a grand time. We hope this helps you relive it again and again.

Sincerely,

John Hughes, Editor

Deseret News staff

Jeffrey D. Allred, Dave Anderton, Timothy A. Aragon, Lynn Arave, Mary Archbold, Stephen J. Ashton, Gerry Avant, Paul G. Barker, Joe Bauman, Marjorie Cortez Behrens, Lee Benson, Bob Bernick Jr., Ray Boren, Lisa Bowen, Michael Brandy, Amy Donaldson Brass, Amy Joi Bryson, Matt Brown, Tim Buckley, Laraine S. Burrows, Jeff Call, Ravell Call, Tammy Carlson, Bob Cazier, Peter Chudleigh, John Clark, Kathryn Clayton, Sterling Clifford, Lois M. Collins, Kent A. Condon, Ron Cook, Jennifer Toomer-Cook, James Cole, David D. Croft, Leah L. Culler, Angela A. Curtis, Larry D. Curtis, Todd Curtis, Lee Davidson, Carolyn Dickson, Lucinda Dillon Kinkead, Jennifer Dobner, James Edward, Daniel B. Edvalson, Vern Elsberry, Rich Evans, Jay Evensen, Zack Van Eyck, Dirk Facer, Geoffrey Fattah, Anne Ferguson, Steve Fidel, Mary Finch, Malin F. Foster, Dave Gagon, Russell J. Gallegos, Jeannine R. Garrett, Chuck Gates, Jody Genessy, Sara Giles, Anna Gill, Barbara Gingery, Ray Grass, Wil Grey, Jennifer Grigg, Alyssa Hickman Grove, Thomas Grover, Nicole Grubbs, Sharon Haddock, Richard D. Hall, Linda A. Hamilton, Linda M. Hamilton, Jeffrey P. Haney,

Laura Hancock, Rodger L. Hardy, Jeremy Harmon, John L. Hart, Tom Hatch, Elyse Hayes, Julie Dockstader Heaps, Mike Heitkamp, Lou Ann Heller, Susan Hermance, Chris Hicks, Greg Hill, Jay Hinton, Craig Holyoak, Rebecca Cline Howard, John Hughes, Jill Huckleberry, W. Lee Hunt, Angelyn Nelson Hutchinson, Jesse Hyde, Scott Iwasaki, Christie L. Jackson, Anne Jacobs, Marina S. O'Neill, Greg Jarrard, Elaine Jarvik, Derek Jensen, Emily Jensen, Jerry Johnston, Sharon Johnson, Stuart Johnson, Loren Jorgensen, Marilyn Karras, Fred Keller, Carrie Kennington, Jo-Ann Wong Kilpatrick, Gregory P. Kratz, Kevin Lee, Seth Lewis, Ivan M. Lincoln, Scott Lloyd, Josh Loftin, Dennis Lythgoe, Sherry S. Madsen, Will Madison, Shane McCammon, Gary M. McKellar, Mauricio Menjivar, John Mitchell, Lisa Montague, Carrie A. Moore, Brady Mortensen, Kari Morandi, Kim Murphy, Alex Nabaum, Jenifer K. Nii, Wendy Nielsen, Jessica Nilsson, Bob Noyce, Wendy Ogata, Jeff Oliver, Jason Olson, Maria Titze, Sylvia Orton, Douglas

Osborn, Val Parsons, Heidi Perry, Valerie Phillips, Scott D. Pierce, Ann Poulson, Pat Poyfair, Jeanne Pratt, Larry Prina, Genelle Pugmire, Colleen Randall, Jim Rayburn, Pat Reavy, Edward Reichel, Jon Ringwood, Doug Robinson, John Robinson, Lisa Riley Roche, Brad Rock, Robert Rogers, Dennis Romboy, Clifton Schmidt, David Schneider, Heidi Scofield, Laura Seitz, Tom Smart, Connie Smith, Brady Snyder, Mike Sorensen, Jerry Spangler, Donna Kemp Spangler, Stephen Speckman, Shaun Stahle, Jason Swensen, Austin Taylor, Scott Taylor, F. Charles Temby III, James Thalman, Linda Thomson, Sharon Thompson, Pete Thunell, Sherry Tingley, Trent Toone, Bob Truelsen, Emmie Truelsen, Heather Tuttle, Diane Urbani, Jolynne Van Valkenburg, Twila VanLeer, Jeff Vice, Carma Wadley, Jim Wall, Brice Wallace, Norma Wagner, Steve Warren, Sarah Jane Weaver, Larry Weist, Angie Welling, Jerry Wellman, Elizabeth White, Pam Whitmore, Susan Whitney, Ashley Williams, Chuck Wing, Linda Woodard, Johanna Workman, Scott G. Winterton

To order additional copies of this book, please call 1 (800) 261-5644.